I CONNECTING: THE SOUL'S QUEST

I CONNECTING:
THE SOUL'S QUEST

BY KRISTINA KAINE

GOLDENSTONE PRESS

HEAVEN & EARTH PUBLISHING

Published by Goldenstone Press and Heaven & Earth Publishing

ISBN-13: 978-0-9779825-3-0
ISBN-10: 0-9779825-3-X

Cover art: Fog & Sunbeams C
Ernest Prim. Image from BigStockPhoto.com

GOLDENSTONE PRESS

GOLDENSTONE PRESS seeks to make original spiritual thought available as a force of
individual, cultural and world revitalization. The press is an integral dimension of the
work of the School of Spiritual Psychology. The mission of the School includes restoring
the book as a way of inner transformation and awakening to spirit. We recognize that
secondary thought and the reduction of books to sources of information and entertainment as the dominant meaning of reading places in jeopardy the unique character of
writing as a vessel of the human spirit. We feel that the continuing emphasis of such a
narrowing of what books are intended to be needs to be balanced by writing, editing
and publishing that emphasizes the act of reading as entering into a magical even mira-
culous spiritual realm that stimulates the imagination and makes possible discerning
reality from illusion in the world. The editoral board of Goldenstone Press is committed
to fostering authors with the capacity of creative spiritual imagination who write in
forms that bring readers into deep engagement with an inner transformative process
rather than being spectators to someone's speculations. A complete catalogue of all our
books may be found at *www.goldenstonepress.com*.

CONTENTS

FOREWORD   5

INTRODUCTION   15

CHAPTER ONE
Human Soul   21

CHAPTER TWO
Human Self: the "I"   49

CHAPTER THREE
Three Soul Faculties: feeling, thinking, willing   91

CHAPTER FOUR
Three Soul Regions: impulse, reasoning, awareness   123

CHAPTER FIVE
Healthy Soul, Strong I-Connection: exercises   157

APPENDIX   183

FOREWORD

This is a radical and remarkable book in many respects. Kristina Kaine, in a clear, straightforward, and simple but sophisticated manner, provides a very new and different view of the life of the soul; that is one aspect. Then, on that basis, she develops an even more clear understanding of the individual human spirit; that is a second aspect. Then, she also proceeds to show us how each of these dimensions intertwine in actual daily living. This is certainly a substantial writing, but it is not for the academic or for the intellectual effete. We find ourselves on every page of what she says. It is a strong book, a strong writing, which, if you take the needed time to study, issues into a different way of living, one that is full of inner excitement that surely expresses itself in behavior and will be readily noticed. You will become more calm, more centered, more able, more heart-oriented, and, most of all, more selfless and interested in others.

Suggesting these qualities result from developing a sense of the I may sound like a string of new age promises, but there is a difference, an enormous difference. New age material is typically conveyed in a way that makes us believe that we already have the capacities to achieve the kinds of qualities stated above, and if we just do one kind of simple practice or another, wear an amulet, hold a crystal, learn the latest approach to the Tarot or some other divination device, the desire will be achieved. The book you hold is not this kind of self-help manual. Rather, you are invited into the riches of becoming a participant-observer in soul and spirit life. It is work, but a very different and new kind of work that can perhaps be characterized as play-work. That is, it is fun, the imagination gets engaged, and you begin to notice things in your daily relationships that make favorable differences.

Because this is a book about soul and spirit life, it seems to me that it might be helpful to clear the ground a bit for readers, as I tried to do above by indicating that this is not another of the more typical self-help books. A second distinction is also necessary. In our time, when the term 'soul' is used, we think of depth psychology—not only the contributions of C.G. Jung, but also James Hillman, Thomas Moore, and the revival of depth psychology in archetypal psychology. This book is also not within that genre. Depth psychology's approach to soul is situated within a Platonic cosmology. I don't want to become lofty here and go into ancient philosophy. However, if we do not know what cosmology we stand within, then we are simply lost and wandering around, homeless. Platonic cosmology is only one aspect of depth psychology, there are other aspects such as Gnosticism, but it is the former that is important here in relation to the writing in this book. For Platonists, soul is a reflection within the human being of archetypal realities existing in the soul realm. These archetypal patterns are the patterning for our actions, our behavior, our emotions and thinking, as well as our pathologies. The standard dictum of depth psychology is "who is the god behind what I am thinking, feeling, or doing."

I made the argument in the preface to Rudolf Steiner's work, *A Psychology of Body, Soul, and Spirit,* and also in my preface to Gehard Wehr's book, *Jung and Steiner: Toward a New Psychology,* that the Platonic background of soul work in psychology needs to be complemented with a more Aristotelian understanding of the soul. Aristotle was more earthly-oriented than Plato, and understood that soul life is formed not only by archetypal realities, but also through the senses, through how we take in the world and how the world lives on within us. It seems obvious, but no one has developed a soul psychology on this basis. The foundation of such a psychology is found in this writing. It is not that what we sense is taken into the soul in any literal way; not, for example as storage of memory images. Rather, how the world around us enters soul life expresses as a contraction or expansion of the soul. And, as our author so well explains it, as a rhythmical dynamic between aversion and attraction, a moving toward those things liked, an expansiveness, and away from those things that are disliked, a contraction. There is much more to it, of course, and it is all beautifully explained in this writing. But, since there are many books now available on the soul, it is always necessary to prepare the reader for the approach to soul being taken. Current writing on soul ranges from the excellent work of many depth psychologists, to a host of writers who use the term without any real understanding. This book expresses a highly developed understanding of soul, but from quite a new perspective.

One dimension of such an understanding of soul that seems to go well beyond what can be found in depth psychology, is that there are levels of soul being. Soul is not just one big bowl of soup. And, in addition, soul is not some thing or quasi-thing, nor is it a theoretical concept. Soul refers to the activity of innerness. And such activity takes a variety of forms that are described as levels, interpenetrating levels of awareness. This book describes all of the levels of soul activity, how they interpenetrate and how we can begin to notice differences in soul dimensions.

You will not find references in this book to archetypal realities because the background is, as I said, more Aristotelian. Others too, have shaped the background of what Kristina Kaine works out, and she is surely in-debted to her mentor, Mario Schoenmaker, a gifted spiritual teacher who lived and worked in Australia. And, there are also resonances of the work of Rudolf Steiner. It is not necessary to have a background in the work of these individuals, but it is right to honor them as Kristina Kaine has done by bringing into practical form what was contained in their vision.

One of the most important descriptions in this writing concerns characterizing soul activity, the innerness of soul, not as something that goes on inside us, but rather the picturing of soul activity as both within us and all around us. We are within soul. Soul thus has the character of a subtle field of forces of a purely non-material kind, not of a bounded entity. This, as you will discover, helps give an account of many different kinds of experience in which we feel the presence of soul 'all around us'.

The field-phenomenology of soul life that is such an important dimen-sion of Kristina Kaine's writing, teaches us to think differently—with more inherent mobility, less literally, less verbally, more with presence than abstraction. Thus, by the time you finish this book, you will find you are not the same person who opened the first page. You have to be actively engaged in developing new capacities as you read the book. It is not a book of information but one of formation, of an awakening of soul into consciousness. Once you have the sense of the actuality of soul, it is really impossible for life to proceed as previously. For one thing, you will want to experiment with this new-found consciousness, become familiar with different levels of soul activity, learn to experience inwardly the difference between the sentient level of soul and the awareness level, for example. Inwardly sensing such differences makes living richer, deeper, and provides ways of working with difficulties, conflicts, and emotions, in ways that therapy never got to because of the lack of soul consciousness in the discipline and profession of psychology.

The chapters on soul life alone make this book exceptional and worth not only reading, but re-reading again and again. But, in a way, the work with soul in this writing is but a prelude to a new and incredibly exciting psychology of spirit that forms the central creative effort of Kristina Kaine.

Individual spirit life expresses itself as the essence of our being and lives as our I. Kristina works through the many senses of the I. In a way, it feels like an awkward term, partly because we are so close to this region of the temple of our being that it is a bit of a shock to see it taken out, so to speak, and examined. Equally, however, we think we are so familiar with our I, for after all it is us, it is who we imagine ourselves to be, that there does not seem to be anything that can be said. The time has come, however, the evolution of consciousness-time, to begin working in an inward way with the I. If we do not, then there will be individuals who will work with the I in highly manipulative ways. This has already happened, for example, with the founding of Scientology. L. Ron Hubbard quite clearly and explicitly developed Scientology and used it as a way of manipulating the individual human spirit. In his foundational book, *The Fundamentals of Thought,* he says:

> The individual man is divisible (separable) into three parts (divisions). The first of this is the spirit, called in Scientology, the *Thetan.* The second of these parts is the Mind. The third of these parts is the Body.
>
> Probably the greatest discovery of Scientology and its most forceful contribution to the knowledge of mankind has been the isolation, description and handling of the human spirit, accomplished in July, 1951, in Phoenix, Arizona. I established along scientific rather than religious or humanitarian lines that the thing which is the person, the personality,

is separable from the body and mind at will and without causing bodily death or mental derangement.

In ages past there has been considerable controversy concerning the human spirit or soul, and various attempts to control man have been effective in view of his almost complete ignorance of his own identity. Latterly spiritualists isolated from the person what they called the astral body, and with this they were able to work for various purposes of their own. In Scientology, the spirit itself was separated from what the spiritualists called the astral body and there should be no confusion between these two things. (page 54)

If you peruse this book by Hubbard, you will find that he is very well aware of the tradition of soul that is also the background of Kristina Kaine's work. I bring this to the fore, not out of any interest in inspiring desire to look into Scientology. I want to make clear what is at stake in the development of a true sense of our I-being. And I want to make clear, that whereas in 1951, Scientology discovered how to manipulate the I-being of persons, with the publication of the book you hold in your hand, Kristina Kaine has restored the *sacredness* of the I-being to its rightful place. She has given us back our individual spirit, not only knowledge of it, but how to care for our I-being, develop it, and become, through this new consciousness, oriented toward being a healing presence in the world.

What is not yet recognized is that most of our sense of our I still remains unconscious. The aspect of our I-being within our consciousness is our ego, though ego also is in intimate connection with our soul, and when the soul lives in contraction rather than expansion, or in an unhealthy rhythm between the two soul motions, the I will express itself in one form or another of negativity—either a sense of inability to face the world or an inflated sense of our abilities, for example.

That Kristina Kaine also sees the critical importance of the harmonious relation between soul and spirit adds a significant dimension to all spiritual work. Even those spiritual traditions that do understand the spiritual significance of the I, such as Anthroposophy, tend to neglect the soul, with the result that the I will always be confused with egotism without the realization that one's spiritual work is ego-centric.

You will find something quite amazing happens when you read the chapters on I-connecting, after having developed a sense of the levels of the soul and their activity. You will, at least momentarily, undergo an actual experience of the deepest and highest sense of the I. And you will be quite astounded! It is like entering a vast, unending loving resource that makes it known to you through immediacy and intimacy of contact. You will feel confident that there is nothing in the world that you cannot meet without a sense of challenge and joy. The experience, of course, quickly slips away, but it is unmistakable, and is the greatest impulse for taking up the exercises described in the writing, which will strengthen this sense of I-being.

Then, there is the further exciting work of learning to place attention within soul and spirit and to begin to recognize how these dimensions of our being can be out of harmony. Many habits you have lived with for years and perhaps have been keeping you out of harmony can begin to be addressed from the place of spirit-I-being. We begin to understand that the activities of soul are autonomous and tend to go their own way until brought into right relation with our I. It is not that the I controls the soul; it does not. It is rather that the relation is like music. That is what is meant by sensing whether soul and spirit are in harmony. When we are in harmony there is a bodily feeling of being in resonance with both soul and spirit; we feel the sense of being within our destiny, a sense of unfolding and changing and, most of all, a sense of being, at the very core of ourselves, creative beings who are called to live every moment within the stance of the creative sense of the I, for that is what the I does—it creates. In the absence of feeling this creative core, we feel pushed into the comfortableness of habit and conformity.

The sense of the creative being of the I has great significance for what goes on in the world beyond ourselves. Not only do we find ourselves other-oriented when we experience the creative presence of the I, we are able to stand against the usurping of the I that is now taking place everywhere in the world. I tried to speak of this usurping of the I in *Freeing the Soul from Fear* as *doubling* which is a pathology of the unconscious I. I mean by doubling that our spirit-being, our I, our spirit-individuality, when it remains unconscious can be taken over and controlled in a radical ways on a mass scale. I did not really have the tools to say what I was trying to say in that writing, and it is only now, with this work of Kristina Kaine's that the predicament and dangers we face in this time of the evolution of consciousness become fully apparent.

It is imperative to recognize the consequences of failing to come to an experience of the I. Doubling is now a rampant pathology in our culture, and consists of cleverness taking the place of creativity, incredible cruelty taking the place of selflessness, complete self-centeredness taking the place of community, and force taking the place of true inner power and authority. We have to ask how it is possible for the cleverness and cruelty that we see with many corporate leaders, politicians, heads of state to exist. When we look at these people, it is easy to see that the person is 'not there', that something has usurped the very core of their being. This pathology cannot be accounted for nor understood by any current psychology because it is not about psychology; it is about the spirit. We have not had a full understanding of the individual spirit and its operation in daily living, until this writing by Kristina Kaine.

Nor have we had any sense whatsoever that we now face a whole host of new pathologies that look like psychopathologies, but they are not. We have yet to recognize that there are pathologies of spirit. Many of them look exactly like psychological difficulties and are being treated as if they were. There is, for example, a kind of anxiety that concerns spirit, not soul. But, many illness such as anorexia, attention deficit disorder, and autism, I think have to do with the spirit. And, in many cases have to do with an awakening of spirit around others and in a culture that does not know how to recognize spirit. In other words, the pathologies of these difficulties lie more on the side of failure to recognize spirit and how to work with spirit in right and healthy ways. One result of this book will be, I hope, new ways of looking at the inner sufferings of individuals.

The indications, though, are clear. The world will continue falling into chaos without the sense of the I as a central light. On the one hand, soul without spirit leads to self-absorption. But the I that goes unconscious leads to cultural chaos. And the I that becomes conscious without working toward the harmony of spirit and soul activity within us is removed, detached, objectively cold. An amazing quality of this writing is that the way to harmony is clearly articulated.

The replacement of the I does not only occur in the drastic manner indicated above. A ground has to be well prepared for that to happen. There has to first be a culture that brings about the complete exteriorization of the I, that is, of the qualities that are inwardly experienced as personality, talents, creativity, goals, and the peculiarities that mark each of us as I. When culture falls to the level where all such qualities are seen to be available "out there", then all that is left of the human being is an easily manipulated unconscious soul life, and an equally vulnerable egotistic sense of the I. Since this condition leaves the soul so vulnerable, there is much inner pain, anxiety, and depression. The pharmaceutical companies feel they can handle those problems, but the real problem with pharmaceuticals is that they dull the sense of the I. And, therapy of the soul, while it can help develop soul consciousness, if it cannot address the sense of the I, results in living in more conscious painfulness without the dimension of joy and enthusiasm that are both exclusively spiritual qualities.

As this writing makes clear, coming into the sense of the I is an evolving process. That is because the kind of consciousness involved is, for each of us, entirely new and thus there are no concepts that can adequately express the experience. This book is perhaps the closest you will find to expressing what happens. The inner sense, however, is still something quite different, lying in the realm of the wordless. If there begins to be an awakening of the I, our author indicates that it may be experienced as anxiety. You may not realize what is happening. This is an exceedingly important moment and it is crucial that it not be interpreted as being primarily a psychological difficulty. It is the moment when we get the first glimpse of the fact that the I is me and not me at the same time. It is certainly not the small 'me', but it is not even 'me' in a larger sense because it is both personal and transpersonal at the same time. If it were merely personal and individual, its awakening would not be frightening because there would be a strong sense of familiarity. But, the awakening involves an equally strong sense of unfamiliarity. One so strong and so central that absolutely everything in your life is thrown into question, but also into a new light. The work is to let the questioning be present without acting on that questioning and develop the capacity of living within this new light of the I. This book is a manual for doing precisely this kind of spiritual work. It is new spiritual work in the world, new because the spiritual being is not 'out there' somewhere to be venerated or addressed, but right here, the central heart of every human being. This book is a guide to coming to be a spiritual human being—something quite different than just being a human being. And it is something very different than a human being doing spiritual things. This book, this writing, marks a most significant turn in inner work, in spiritual work, and in our very way of being in the world.

—ROBERT SARDELLO

INTRODUCTION

The need for an understanding of soul and spirit

The deep longing to know ourselves takes us on many quests. A feeling of emptiness often accompanies our achievements when the fruits of our life do not satisfy us as we expected they would. Global affairs, especially the many natural and man-made disasters, give rise to despair. Our inclination is to look outside ourselves to understand these issues. Could we be looking in the wrong direction? Would greater self-knowledge change the way we see what is happening in the world? Could understanding our soul and spirit make a difference?

We are at a crisis point in evolution, a pivotal time for humanity.

This book explains that we are beings of body, soul and spirit and that, for too long, knowledge of our soul and spirit has been ignored. Do we have a complete picture of a car by describing its shell, its shape and colour, while ignoring the engine, mechanics and the driver? The truth is that our physical body without our soul and spirit is just an empty shell. There is a good case to make that, because we think of our total being as just a physical body, we are at such a crisis point.

Take a long thoughtful look at what is happening in the world today. Why are youth suicides increasing? How can we explain the rise of new and sometimes untreatable diseases? Why are people turning to the past for fundamental religious values which can foster terrorism, or at least undermine free will? Is it fear of the future which makes the past more attractive than perhaps it should be? Change is everywhere. Scientists regularly make discoveries which lead them to rethink their hypotheses about what it means to be a complete human being. Understanding our inner world can help us deal with the rapidly changing outer world.

This book is for all people interested in experiencing firsthand what is hidden in human nature. Knowledge of the soul and spirit is not complicated. By using the guidelines set out in this book it will become clear that all we are required to do is to become more observant in life. Then we need to think deeply about our observations.

We think other people's thoughts.

Our thinking has become lazy because we are spoon fed so many ideas by the media and this undermines our ability to think. Words and phrases are often used in common speech today with little understanding of what they mean; they sounded good on the television. The police have discovered that modern criminals model their life on movies like The Godfather instead of the reverse situation where writers base their scripts on the clever behaviour of criminals. How many millions of people now experience life through reality television? They have been hoodwinked into thinking that other people's lives are infinitely more interesting than their own. Furthermore, are we aware of the way advertising agencies define our standards and values through advertising campaigns on billboards and in the media?

This crisis can be understood differently if we look more closely at what is happening in our own being. If more people started today to discover the inner nature of their own soul and its relationship to their spirit, their interest in reality television may dwindle. It would be seen for the escapism that it is. Not only would their life and their social environment be more captivating; the voyeurism of reality television would no longer attract them as it used to.

We are at a point in evolution where changes happening in our own soul and spirit, which change our consciousness, can shed some light onto today's crisis.

What is our soul? What is our spirit?

So, if we have a soul, where is it and what does it do? And what is our spirit? To be able to truly understand ourselves we need to build a picture of the place of our soul and our spirit in our being.

Have you ever looked into a coffin to see the lifeless body lying there? It is then that we realise that the personality we knew is no longer present. We usually recognise the face and then we are hit by the fact that there is much more to this person than their physical body. Yet science, demanding scientific proof, continues to ignore this part of us that is obviously present while we live and leaves when we die.

In essence, our soul is an activity within us which is created by the way we feel, think, and act. Obviously when we die we stop feeling, thinking and acting and it is this activity that leaves the shell of our body at death. Apart from that, we must ask, "Who is feeling, thinking and acting?" The answer is I am. This "I" or 'self' is the name we call ourselves when we refer to ourselves. This is our human spirit.

Our "I", this 'self', experiences life through our soul and our body. The "I" is the artist, the soul his work of art and the body is the canvas. Similarly, the "I" is the gardener, the garden is our soul and the soil is our body.

Why study our soul and spirit?

The question is: How do we connect these things up within ourselves? When we become more conscious of how we paint the canvas or tend to the garden, we have a new lease on life. The new consciousness wakes up our soul and we become aware of the guiding, directing, 'all-seeing' presence of the painter or gardener; our spirit which in this book we refer to as our "I".

We all want to understand ourselves better, we all want to know how to get along with others more harmoniously, and we all want to have loving relationships. Knowledge of our soul and spirit holds the key to developing these aspects of our lives.

The rise in popularity of self-development systems is witness to the yearning within many people to understand their being more fully. Psychology (the study of the soul) being one of the most popular courses of study today testifies to this. Yet how many psychologists are aware of the specific activity of the soul? Furthermore, the rise of so-called mental disorders, especially in young children, and the increasing use of medication for these, points to an urgency to unravel some more of the mysteries of the human being. A suburban mother, when interviewed for a current affairs programme, described her ten year old son on medication for Attention Deficit Disorder as an empty shell with no soul. This speaks of a growing awareness in the population in general that we are more than just a body, just a shell.

Knowledge of soul and "I" assists to understand self and others.

The question stands: Do we continue to point outside ourselves to the cause of all the personal and social issues we face today or could we look more closely into our own being? After all, our actions and attitudes contribute to society and create the culture we live in. It is the sum total of everyone's ideas and actions that create society. As we become more conscious of this, our understanding of self and others grows. This, in turn, assists us to make sense of emerging characteristics in the human race. The human race evolves in consciousness; we do not think the same way that we thought even fifty years ago. Understanding how soul, spirit and body function and interact not only increases our own awareness of self, it helps us make better sense of our place in this increasingly complex and developing world.

This fundamental issue that the soul, and its relationship to our spirit, is a work in progress, has escaped the attention of many of those who study the human being. By factoring in knowledge of how the soul has evolved over the past centuries, and that it also matures in each human being differently, new understandings can be developed.

The importance of the I-connection.

Our consciousness arises from the relationship between our soul and our "I". By understanding them, and becoming aware of the way they work, we can change our consciousness. Do we think differently today than we did a thousand years ago? We can trace an evolution of consciousness throughout the whole of history that reveals that we do. With an understanding of the soul and the "I" we can also trace a changing relationship between our soul and our "I". Today, it is important for us to work on the I-connection in our soul. Our "I" can only connect up with our soul if we become aware of the activity of our soul. Do we have full control of our feelings? Do we use our thinking to the full extent? Are our actions always purposeful?

Discovering our soul and spirit is a personal quest

This book will lead you along a path of self-discovery and will assist you to explore and experience your soul and spirit yourself. We can only really understand and become aware of our soul and spirit through personal experience. Working with the material in this book you will be surprised how easy it is to see the soul and spirit at work in yourself and in others. Many things will fall into place like pieces of a jigsaw.

These guidelines for the discovery of your own unique soul and spirit are easy to follow. Recommendations are given that can be integrated simply in daily life. The results are immediate and continual!

Working with this book

As you are reading and exploring the themes and exercises outlined, we recommend that you keep a personal journal. This is a very helpful way to record observations of our soul-I responses to daily life, to map our unique soul-I expressions and to record changes and set goals for further change. This book gives guidance for a refreshing new approach to charting such change. Further assistance can be found by attending Quest of the Soul workshops or using the Quest of the Soul personal workbook. Information about these can be found on the website www.soulquesting.net.

Chapter 1: Human Soul

Identifying our soul

Before we can explore the nature of our "I" we must first understand the activity that is our soul.

Our quest is not for a soul-mate but to be mates with our soul.

How can we discover our soul and experience that we are more than just a physical body? It is a great exercise to ask a few people if they have a soul. After a long pause many people say, "Yes". Then ask them where it is. Some people wave their hands vaguely around their heart and neck. Others think that their soul is not connected to them, that it has to do with their family or their environment. Many others think of their soul as a thing associated with death, that it leaves when the body dies, but they have few ideas about what it does while the body lives. Still others think that the soul has something to do with religion, and if they reject religion therefore, they conclude, they probably don't have a soul.

There are, however, an increasing number of people who are beginning to experience their soul and "I" and they are able to explore how they actually work within their daily life. The author is one of these people; and in this book I invite you to join me in my exploration of a more complete human being-ness.

The signposts along this road can be quite confusing because of the misunderstandings of the soul and the "I". While this book presents a framework, it does not intend to negate other systems of understanding; it should shed light on them. Still, there will always be some resistance because we live in a world where physical, scientific proof is the ultimate end. By exploring something that we cannot physically dissect will always be viewed by some to be entering a sphere of fantasy or fiction.

The core functions of the soul are feeling, thinking and willing.

The soul is definitely not fantasy or fiction. The soul is not something vague and nebulous. The very tools that science relies on are the core functions of the soul. These tools are *thinking, action* and, for science to some extent, *feeling.* If scientific thought accepted, rather than rejected, these basic human functions as soul functions, if its approach was from the side of probability rather than implausibility, some surprising results could be revealed.

Feeling, thinking and willing are the core functions of the conscious human being. It is the way we use feeling, thinking and our will that reveals the colour of our soul. As we grow and mature it is possible to use them in more refined ways according to the strength of our I-connection. The peak human experience is to be able to use them with clarity and awareness. Yet for the most part many of us only use them in a dreamy, semi-conscious or unconscious way.

This book is written to assist you to explore these aspects of yourself and personally test them for yourself. You will be able to decide whether they are valid or not through self-observation. Even if the results are not immediately convincing, after continued consideration people are becoming more aware of the activity of their soul in their daily life. They also discover the rewards of this knowledge which are confidence, awareness and calmness among other things.

As you read on you will discover many ways to become conscious of your own individual soul and I-connection. With this knowledge we can become more aware of the way others act and this can immediately give us insights into the way we act. In this case, the other person acts like a mirror for us to understand some of the semi-conscious things that we do. This insight into ourselves, by ourselves, is empowering and liberating, and the new awareness cannot help but change us.

What is most refreshing about this way of understanding our soul and I-connection is that it doesn't introduce a mysterious new system which uses specific jargon. Human functioning is described in every day terms, so that we can simply become more aware of what we already do. In this awareness, without jargon or extensive or difficult exercises, we will come to know ourselves more intimately.

The best way to begin our exploration is to consider a newborn baby.

Are we born with a soul?

Newborn babies are absorbed in three core activities; to cry and to eat and to excrete. They can't focus their eyes, they can't smile and they can't co-ordinate their limbs. Why is this? The answer to this question carries the key to understanding the soul.

Usually our soul is not connected with our body when we are born. Observe a newborn baby closely and you will see that the human soul connects up with us when, as babies, our eyes are able to focus. The time for this soul connection can vary from at the time of birth to many weeks after birth. Some babies accept their soul easily and others do not—this can be observed by their amount of restlessness.

Newborns do reveal a personality shining through and in those early weeks and months, much time is spent by parents analysing their personality and their temperament. Personality is not the expression of the soul but rather of the human spirit. This is an important distinction to make as we begin to explore these hidden aspects of our selves.

Our soul is coloured by our physical and social environment.

As we grow from children to adults our soul life is moulded. We each have specific ways of feeling, thinking and acting. This moulding is influenced by many factors including the country we grow up in. Scientists are now discovering that they cannot identify 'race' in our DNA. Instead of 'race' we can identify different soul moods in the different places of the world. These soul moods are influenced by many conditions, especially climate, which has a deep effect on the way we think and form our habits and values. Then, some people are closely bonded to the national soul mood; others feel at home in whatever country they visit or live. Also, those living in the city differ from those living in the county. Living in specific suburbs within a city also affects our soul. The reasons for this will become more obvious when we look at the different regions of soul.

This is where we find the keys to understanding the soul and its different expressions across the globe.

Our spirit expresses itself through our soul.

Anchored deep in the core of our soul is the essence of each human being. The Psychoanalyst Carl Jung identified it as the Self. In this book we refer to the 'self' as the "I", which, as discussed earlier, has an evolving connection with all the levels of our being. This "I" can also be called the human spirit. For a clear understanding of ourselves it is important to differentiate the "I" from the soul, a distinction that is easily overlooked or obscured. It is the "I" that connects up with the soul by using feeling, thinking and willing as its tools. When the "I" does not connect up with the soul our feeling, thinking and willing are automatic and unconscious. The "I" is the musician who tries to play the instrument that is our soul; the strings of the instrument are feeling, thinking and willing.

The key factor about the "I" is that it can express itself in a range of ways from being egotistical/self-centred at one end to being totally selfless at the other end. We will look in detail at the way the "I" works after we have a clearer understanding of our soul.

As we build a picture of how our spirit interacts with our soul, it is important to include in this picture how our soul interacts with our body. While we describe these parts of us as if they are separate it is crucial to see them as an integrated whole. Our task is threefold:

1. to become more conscious of how they work;
2. to become more aware of whether they co-operate or not; and
3. to realise how they work differently for each person.

This is the wonderful thing about soul-I knowledge; it reveals how we are all on the same journey but take an individual approach. Someone famously said, "We are all the same but different".

By becoming mates with our soul we will be less inclined to look outside ourselves for a soul-mate. The new relationship between our "I" and our soul will change the way we relate to others. It will also change the way we feel about ourselves, making us more content and self-sufficient. Our relationships with our partners and friends can be affected. We could find that the growth in our awareness, if it is not matched by our partners and friends, will put a strain on our relationships. Those without relationships will have a different motivation for seeking committed relationships and friendships. With these thoughts in mind we can delve more deeply into the nature of the soul.

What is our soul?

It is within our soul that the human abilities of feelings, thoughts and intentions (will/action) are developed and ordered. They are the basis for our consciousness. Remember that it is our "I" that is feeling, thinking and forming our intentions. We feel, think and act according to the way our "I" is connected to our soul; specifically according to the strength of our I-connection. In this respect we can say that our "I" is the 'eye' of our soul. The question is, how strong is our vision, and how blind are we? This is the measure of our consciousness.

Our consciousness is expressed using our physical body, primarily our brain. Hippocrates observed that the brain was the messenger of consciousness, not the consciousness itself. So our brain is a tool through which we express our consciousness. The livelier our consciousness is the better its vehicle. We also express our consciousness in the gestures of our hands, our facial expressions, and also our posture. All this is influenced by the condition of our soul.

The soul takes time to connect after we are born.

To further develop our understanding, consider that our soul gradually connects with our body after birth. A newborn is not conscious until its soul has taken hold of its body. We can observe the changes in a new-born baby as its soul begins to take hold. First the eyes become alert and gradually they take on their intended colour. For instance, all babies are born with steel grey or dark blue eyes; they may stay grey or blue or turn green, hazel, or brown in the first months of life. After a while the baby develops the ability to communicate with its facial expressions, especially with its ability to smile.

We can also see in the developing child how it strengthens its abilities of feeling, thinking and intention. It doesn't take much to work out which ability it develops first. It is through feeling that a baby communicates its needs to its mother. This feeling can even be mistaken for will, or can even be called a feeling-will. At this stage, the child's ability to think is not developed, and it cannot control its actions. This is particularly notice-able in the uncoordinated movements of its arms and legs. As mentioned earlier, excessive wriggling is often a sign that the baby has to work harder to assimilate its soul.

Our soul continues to integrate into our body during the first few years of life. This process can be measured by the degree of consciousness in a child. In fact, an adult who is not so conscious may have a loose con-nection with their soul. The fact that people who are autistic don't have the ability to smile indicates that there is a problem with the connection between their soul and their body. It is beyond the scope of this book to explore autism; however, knowledge of the soul and the "I" could provide some answers.

Where is our soul?

Our soul is all around us yet it is our inner world.

Our soul is all around us like an ocean or a cloud and we exist within it. It is not only inside our physical body as people may think. Nor, as we can see from the above descriptions, are we simply a physical body. Rather, our physical body sits within our soul and we are beings of body, soul and spirit. We can say that our body houses, or is the vehicle for, our soul but as our soul is a collection of forces, feelings and thoughts, the physical body is not a barrier to it.

We experience this if we enter a room where there has been tension or an argument; we even say that the atmosphere is tense. This tension exists in the souls of the people involved and does indeed fill the space in the room. There is also a lot of truth in the saying, "we lost it" when we lose our temper. We allow our anger to spill out into our environment unchecked. This is good reason to take more responsibility for our feelings, knowing how they can affect those around us.

While we can say that our soul is our inner world, at the same time we can see that its activity moves around us as well. From the following diagram we can see that it is our physical body that swims within our soul, not the reverse. If we imagine that we are swimming in the ocean of our feelings, thoughts and intentions, we can see that we are within our soul and at the same time it is our inner world. In fact, we could say that the activity of our soul can be found where our inner life connects with our environment.

Picture the soul extending fifty to sixty centimetres (18-24 inches) from our body. Remember that the cloud is the activity of our soul stimulated by our feelings, thoughts and intentions. The outline shows that the physical body is both inside the soul and interpenetrated by it. The way the soul connects with our body varies from person to person and according to the prevailing conditions in our life.

How does our soul work?

Our soul is not a 'thing', but an activity.

It is easier to understand how we exist within our soul when we experience how our soul is not a 'thing' like a physical object, but is an activity.

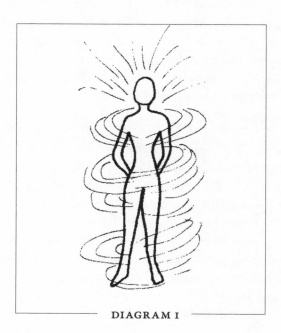

DIAGRAM I

If we place ourselves within this activity of continual feeling, thinking and intention we can experience the forces of our soul as they rise and fall, ebb and flow and swirl within us and around us. By imagining that we swim in this ocean of forces created by feeling, thinking and intention (willing), then we can really feel ourselves within our soul and cease to think about our soul as an object.

Take a moment to experience yourself looking from within to what is around you. Remain connected to yourself and feel your connection with the external world and the other people in it. You will notice how, at times, you like to be withdrawn, and at other times, more fully connected to your environment. This awareness provides a greater opportunity for harmony within our being. We can become more aware of how we remain connected or retreat in certain situations.

Now, turn your attention to this private ocean of your thoughts, feelings and intentions; this is your inner, private world. To fully experience this, ask yourself the question: Who is thinking? Who is feeling? It is, of course, the "I". The way we personally experience these activities forms the individual expression of our soul. Some of us feel more, some think more and some like to take action and some others do not.

It is also important to become aware that quite often our soul and "I" do not work in harmony. Our soul can work automatically out of years of habitual behaviour and resist the influence from the "I". When looking at how our soul works we must become increasingly aware that it is the "I" that brings the harmony, balance and control.

The soul has several core activities and modes of operation.

At the core of our soul we find two basic expressions; laughter and tears. In joyous laughter our soul expands, it feels enlarged, encompassing. When we cry because of pain or sadness our soul contracts, it feels small, insignificant and overwhelmed. When we cry it is as if our soul has been squeezed, when we laugh we float like a balloon.

At its foundation the basic soul activities are found in love and hate, wishing and longing, satisfaction and dissatisfaction, judgment and consequences. When we experience the extremes of any of these we know that it is our soul at work and not our spirit. Our spirit brings the balance between the two extremes. Within our soul it is as though a pendulum were swinging from one extreme to the other as we think our thoughts, experience our feelings and act out our intentions. It is good for us to experience the extremes, the light and the dark side if you like, but then always to allow the "I" to create harmony.

Through all this activity, we find three perpetual processes occurring in our soul:

1. polarisation, then;
2. improvement, followed by;
3. change or metamorphosis.

We can become *polarised* between love and hate. We can then *adapt* ourselves so that our dissatisfaction becomes satisfaction. Then we can *change* completely so that we cease to long for what no longer has purpose; in the same way that a butterfly won't nibble away at a leaf as it needed to when it was a caterpillar.

What is important is that there is movement occurring in the soul. It is even more imperative that our soul is awake. For the most part our soul dreams through all these activities, as we will discuss in a while.

Through soul awareness we can change our habits.

The quality of our soul depends on the sum total of our life's experiences. Through each step we take in life we mould the way we feel, think and act. Our responses to life create patterns of behaviour which become habits. The later the stage in life, usually the more difficult it is to change these habits. However, by becoming aware of the different activities of our soul we see that these habitual patterns are simply combinations of past feeling, thinking and willing. This, in itself, can assist us to do things differently.

I was at a Catholic seminary attending a retreat and on Friday they served fish for lunch. I said, "Oh, yes, Catholics eat fish on Friday." The lady serving said, "We don't do that any more, but we always have fish on Friday".

How aware are we of all the unconscious habits that make up our self-expression? Obviously many of them are useful so that we can get through the day, but many are not. What is important is that we become more conscious of our feelings, thoughts, and actions.

Many of the self-help formulas espoused in the world would have us work blindly on ourselves. They encourage us to force change rather than understand *what* we are changing. This can do more damage than good. This book will assist you to become conscious of your own unique patterns, and in your awareness, change can come about organically without harm.

To become aware of the workings of our soul we can re-examine and re-experience all our previous values and experiences. Not that we should sit down and make a task out of this. We simply decide to become more conscious of the foundation of our values as we go about our daily life. Why do we think in a certain way? Why do we have the feelings that we do in some situations? Perhaps we learned them from our parents and it would be more suitable if we developed our own way of thinking and feeling. Why do we take an instant dislike to something, or why do we love certain things? These responses can often be linked to a point in the past when we were happy or sad. We can trace backwards through our life to discover the time when a response was born. The awareness of the real catalyst can restore balance in our soul. Thoughtfully observing how we act in a situation, and comparing how we act differently sometimes, can also give us valuable insights into the way our soul works.

Observe how we connect to the outside world.

By thinking more about how we move around in the world, interact with others, and take in things from our environment we discover how the contents of our soul are formed. We can describe the process quite simply: we take things into our soul through our senses. In this way the outside world enters into our soul and we digest the sensations and images and make something of them.

For example, if we see a person we know, we bring forward a similar image from our memory so that we can identify the person – otherwise we could not recognise them. We experience thoughts and feelings about similar images, which assist us to decide how to act in response to the person we see. If we like them we will move towards them; if we don't like them we will seek to avoid them. Sometimes we think we recognise a person only to discover when we speak to them that they simply resemble someone we know. The embarrassment we feel is a response in our soul to attributing feelings and thoughts to the wrong image.

The way we connect to the world assists our soul to acquire wisdom.

When we receive an impulse or an impression from the outside world through our senses, we *think* about it logically, and harmonise it with our *feelings*. All this occurs in our soul where we also form *intentions* which prompt us to express ourselves back into the world. This is rhythmic soul breathing which is referred to later on, see diagram 1.3.

In our soul, we decide what is useful and what is harmful. For example, if we see a dark cloud in the sky, the impression enters our senses and logical thinking tells us there is a good chance that it will rain. Our first *thought* may be that we don't have an umbrella. *Feelings* arise in response to these thoughts, for example, annoyance that our new clothes will be ruined. These feelings have to harmonise with our thoughts. When we become fully aware of the situation we will have developed a plan of *action*. We may have a cup of coffee or browse in a bookshop while we wait for the rain to stop; or go to buy an umbrella. This is the perpetual process that is our soul acquiring wisdom.

However, there can be glitches in the process. It is possible for a person to see something and not know what it is or what to make of it, so the image does not increase understanding in the moment. When we see an event but we do not understand it, this indicates that the event does not enter our soul – through our body we observe it and can make nothing of it simply because it remains outside our soul. Such things happen when a person is very old, on medication, or in a state of emotional distress. The processes of the soul are disconnected.

There are other situations which point to the nature of our soul, for instance, when we see something for the first time. Seeing something for the first time means that our soul has nothing to compare it with. The picture enters our senses and we can find no similar picture so we do not know what to make of it. This is the experience people had when two aeroplanes were deliberately flown into the World Trade Center in New York on September 11, 2001; or when an Australian Aboriginal woman saw a truck for the first time and thought it as a moving rock.

Another good illustration of this is told about Charles Darwin's voyage to South America. They anchored the ship, the Beagle, and went ashore. It was a large ship, larger than the natives had ever experienced before. A sailor asked a native what he thought about his ship and the native replied through the interpreter, "What ship? All I see is a large bird out on the water." These examples explain the soul's processes perfectly. The soul can be compared to a big database processor which searches and filters its data continually.

Our soul on auto-pilot

One of the first things we discover when we become more aware of our soul is how little we have been aware of it until now. We realise that for the most part we experience the life of our soul as if we were asleep and dreaming. Therefore, our awareness is often misty, dream-like. This is natural. When we become aware of our feeling, thinking and willing, we wake up our soul and become more conscious of how our "I" interacts with it. We will discuss this in much more detail in the next chapters.

Our soul has a life of its own.

Primarily, it is our soul that shapes the way we operate in the world. By becoming more conscious of our soul's natural processes we can influence them instead of them influencing us. We can become increasingly able to interrupt our automatic processes and responses. For the most part, it is usually only after the event that we realise that we could have responded differently. What usually happens is that our past memories rise up and they can have an automatic effect on our response to a situation. For example, we may look at a tree and respond to its beauty, or we may feel fearful when we remember that we fell out of such a tree as a child; or without conscious memory, the smell of paint may give us a headache because as a child we smelt the paint as we fell off a ladder and bumped our head.

We are definitely not always conscious of what is working within our soul. Sometimes the independent activity in our soul can take us by surprise. For example, we may be working in a routine way with no apparent concerns then suddenly have a terrible argument with a fellow worker; or we may suddenly feel anxious and not know why. When this happens, the activity of our soul has taken over and our responses are habitual or unconscious. When we become more conscious of these responses to life we can choose to act differently. Or, simply by being conscious of the responses logic tells us that it is not reasonable to act that way.

If we remind ourselves that our soul is all around us, in us and through us, it is easy to see that there are many forces that can influence us – from within and from without. The mood of a co-worker can trigger unconscious responses in our soul. When we are not conscious of the processes that take place—minute by minute!—our soul chugs along as if on auto-pilot, the *driver* is asleep. These are the moments when we act habitually or when we drift off in a reverie; pictures arise in our mind, mental images which can be caused by the chain of events happening at random around us; even other people's thoughts can seep into our soul and affect us.

Consider what happens when we travel on public transport; a stream of mental images flow into us. These mental images then live in our soul and can even take on a life of their own. If we are not paying attention we can find ourselves reacting to something and then wonder what happened. An example of this outside influence would be when we start the day feeling in a good mood, then gradually throughout the day our mood dampens and our tolerance declines. Through awareness of the activity of our soul this is less likely to happen. If the *driver*, which is our "I", is in charge, we will be much more conscious of what is influencing us and we will be able to consciously decide when and how to respond to situations.

How to recognise the activity of our soul

The activities of our soul life include; impressions, perceptions, images, thinking, reasoning, judgments, instincts, impulses, wishes, intentions, hates, loves, emotion, feeling, beauty, joy, pleasure, mindfulness, remembering, inner conflict and tension, anxiety, sadness, vulnerability and loss of control. When any of these things occur in our life they are happening in our soul regions.

Mental images are food for the soul.

The core need of our soul is for mental images, it is like the body's need for nourishment. The forming of mental images within our soul is a complex task involving the whole of the life of our soul. It is helpful to know that it is not when our soul is active but rather when our soul life comes to rest that we actually form an image or picture. If our soul cannot form new mental images boredom sets in. So there is a need for a period of stimulation followed by a period of reflection. Too much stimulation or too much reflection means that the soul is not 'breathing'.

Action is instigated by the soul.

When we act in the world, the motive for action lives in our soul, then at a certain point it takes hold of the body to make the body move. Our movements are not instigated by our limbs acting like a set of levers but rather by our soul sending instructions to our body. Other experiences like hunger and thirst originate in our body as *drives* and enter our soul where decisions are made to satisfy them. The decisions about how to satisfy them comes from the soul. The more awake the soul and more connected our "I", the better the decision. See chapter 3 and diagram 3.3 for more about this.

Heightened experiences usually happen in our spirit. When we see something breathtakingly beautiful it is the eternal quality of our "I" that is usually affected. As we experience the difference between our soul and our "I" we realise that through our spirit we can calm the waters of our soul.

Our soul is as broad and deep as the ocean and our experiences can therefore have a vast range; especially consider love and hate and all the gradients in between. Love itself can be experienced in a higher, refined way or in a lower selfish way. We can therefore talk about lower and higher soul levels within the three different soul regions. The regions of the soul are connected to feeling, thinking and willing. The levels refer to higher and lower levels of feeling, thinking and acting. More detail about these levels and regions can be found later on in this chapter and in chapter 4. When the lower levels of our soul rule this gives rise to expressions of self-centeredness, ego, untruthfulness, vindictiveness, anger. Higher soul experiences involve clarity of awareness, moments of wisdom and a sense of unity with others.

The natural inclination of the soul is to live in its feelings.

When considering the three activities that are our soul, feeling, thinking and intention, we notice that the soul has a natural tendency to bob around in the feeling regions because it requires less effort. In this dreamy state we are usually unmotivated to think or to act. It is through becoming conscious that we jog ourselves to think or to do something. As we start observing our soul more closely, we find that our soul responds to our environment in the following three ways.

1. OUR SOUL FEELS MORE COMFORTABLE WITH THE FAMILIAR. There is a sense of peace when we feel comfortable. For example, we like coming home after a holiday—our environment may not be as smart as the luxury hotel we stayed in, and our bed less comfortable, but we are pleased to be home. This is because our soul feels most comfortable with what it has experienced in the past, what it is familiar with. There are even strong instincts in our soul to remove anything new, anything that disturbs the comfortable patterns. To embrace something new requires effort. Can we muster the energy it takes to do things differently? Changing the way we do the smallest task or making a larger change such as breaking an emotional pattern, or moving into the unknown with courage, takes immense effort. However, when our soul engages with something new, we have an opportunity to experience the activity of our soul.

2. OUR SOUL IS DRAWN TO LIVE IN THE NEW. Today, in this modern world, there are some people who always want to live in the new; they want to participate in the latest ideas and experience new sensations and have new possessions. They are often called 'early adopters' or 'first-movers'. This can also mean that past experiences are not valued and do not become a basis on which to build a future. This is the soul mood that motivates us to go shopping, seeking out the new, whether we need it or not. Marketing companies seek to attract the attention of this soul mood.

3. OUR SOUL ALLOWS THE OLD AND THE NEW TO MEET IN THE PRESENT. There is a wonderful saying: "Today is tomorrow's yesterday. Make the most of the present." The person who can move back and forth in the two streams of the old (past familiar) and the new (future unfamiliar) in a balanced way, is one who is awakening their soul and moving forward within the ongoing evolution of consciousness.

The following diagram shows how the present is that point where the past and future intersect. Many people do not live in the present. The present moment takes into account both the past we are moving away from and the future that comes toward us.

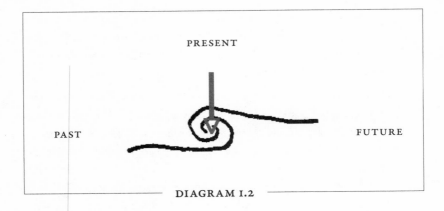

DIAGRAM I.2

The natural inclination of the soul to live in its feelings is because the feeling level of the soul was the first to be developed. Our feelings, when left to their own devices, automatically pull us towards the past. We can look into history to see how the soul and "I" have developed over time. This may also assist us to see what lies ahead for our on-going development of consciousness.

History reveals the presence of soul and spirit

Over time people change; we evolve, not simply in a Darwinian sense, which tracks our physical changes, but also by growing in soul and spirit. Recorded history is the benchmark for this evolution of consciousness. We do not think the same way today as we did fifty or one hundred years ago. Could we possibly think the way we did five hundred years ago and still navigate modern society? Those who question whether we have a soul or not, will find history a fruitful place to search for the signs of man's evolving soul and spirit.

The place of the soul has moved from the tribe to the individual.

Historically, it is not too difficult to see that the soul has evolved from a group expression to a personal expression, from the tribe to the individual. We can see the evidence of this if we look towards the world's indigenous groups as they deal with the effects of this. One Australian

Aboriginal woman recently said that if her people behaved the way they were behaving towards the children of the tribe twenty years ago they would have been killed.

We can also observe that as the soul moves closer to the personal it also internalises what it previously experienced externally. The rise of psychology, which in some ways can be seen to have replaced religion, reveals the change of focus from the outer God to the inner self.

This internalising also marks a trend from the selfless group consciousness to the selfish. 'Selfishness' can actually be seen as an appropriate stage in the vast human journey from tribe to individual; from selfless to selfish ('me') and forward to individualised selflessness (not altruism). Careful observation will reveal that at present we are very much in the 'me' phase where individuality can be taken to the wrong extreme.

Gender equality is another example of the changing consciousness of our time. Consider the changes that women's liberation has brought about; women developing their own career, and sharing the responsibility of home and children with their partner or domestic assistant. Also, men managing the household while their wives develop their career. This also points to the pivotal times we live in. Through understanding the role of our soul and spirit we can map the journey forward; a journey which can be seen portrayed by great and mysterious images like a virgin birth or a man nailed to a cross who is described as dying for all.

This picture of the evolving soul reveals that there was a time when our soul was not directly controlled by us. Then the soul belonged to the tribe under the direction of the tribal elder. By all indications the soul began to 'internalise', and our inner life began to arise, around the time of the ancient Egyptians. At this time we can see the development of a sophisticated culture, a culture that clearly distinguished the human being from animals.

At the time of Buddha the focus was deeply on the individual and the external world was seen as an illusion. Today, scientists say that the only reality is the external world of matter. They also say that mind is the body because they cannot prove otherwise in their laboratory. At the same time, these scientists say that they cannot explain the deepest human wonder which is love.

If we start from the premise of accepting that we do have a soul and a spirit, rather than denying it, we discover that we can logically explain some of the things scientists cannot replicate by 'mechanical' means. Mapping out the evolution of consciousness reveals the place and purpose of the soul and spirit in the lives of human beings.

Aristotle: first to identify different soul functions

To have a better understanding of the soul, it is good to build a picture of its evolution. We can chart the development of the constitution and disposition of our soul. We can become aware of our changing consciousness and our relationship to the external world which itself changes. We can see that this activity that is our soul operates in many different ways in each one of us. Our differences and our similarities can be understood if we consider the nature of the three regions of soul first described by Aristotle (born 384 BC).

Aristotle describes three soul qualities.

Aristotle was among the first to write about the human soul. Prior to this, knowledge of the soul (as far as it was developed) was instinctual. Several hundred years before the time of Christ, Aristotle described the soul as having three qualities and he called these three soul qualities: *Orektikon, Kinetikon*, and *Dianoetikon*.

1. *Orektikon* refers to desires, appetites, sensations, impulses: These things occur in the first soul region where *drives* and *desires* are given dignity. Drives (example, the urge to eat) and desires (example, longings and passions) originate in our physical body. As they rise up into our soul regions they are moderated so that they can be satisfied in a dignified way. We can reach a good understanding of this process by comparing the drives of an animal and a human. For example, an animal's drive to eat may be ennobled by a human desire to create aesthetically pleasing food. This region is the gateway to the soul; in this region we receive the impulses, sensations and impressions from the body and from the outside world through the senses. The soul activity of *feeling* is associated with this region.

2. *Kinetikon* means to set in motion, to try every way, reasoning: In this region we think about what came to us through the senses. Our thinking is set in motion and it tries to recreate a harmony of relationship between the new things that enter our soul with what is already in our soul. This is a process similar to the resolving of musical chords or progressive mathematical patterns. We say that, "something doesn't add up" or that we "can't make sense of something" when our thinking is in motion but remains unresolved. This soul region is concerned with reasoning and logic—*thinking* has its base in this region.

3. *Dianoetikon* is about intentions, our will, to be minded or purpose to do: After we have used our reasoning ability, we can come to a point of awareness, of wisdom. It is in this soul region that we develop our intentions, our volition and we reach a resolution that we can act on. It is from this point that we can act from the wise freedom of our own being rather than from the influence of others. This is the highest region of our soul which we are currently developing. All intentions arise out of the force of our *will*.

Aristotle actually spoke of five members of the soul. In addition to the impulse soul (*orektikon*), the reasoning soul (*kinetikon*), and the awareness soul (*dianoetikon*), he included two lower regions; the plant-like soul and the animal-like soul. The plant-like soul is the area where our *drives* arise; the urge to eat or drink for the well-being of our physical body. From the animal-like soul arise the *desires* that motivate us to seek satisfaction of our drives and passions. The higher regions of our soul, according to how they are developed, give human dignity to how these drives and desires are satisfied.

Our main *driving* forces are found in the forces of growth, reproduction and metabolism—the forces of survival. It is when these *drives* unite with our *desires* that they enter the region of our soul. Our soul begins to engage in the process at this point. If we are able to loosen the grip of desires in our soul then they become wishes and longings which, given the opportunity, the "I" can fulfil through the forces of our will. The more the "I" is involved the more nobly we will express ourselves. This will be explored in more detail in chapter 3 and diagram 3.3.

We are personalising what previously belonged to the tribe.

Those who study writing, such as Aristotle's, thoughtfully realise that the soul was being written about then because consciousness of the soul was changing. This change aroused a need in humanity at the time to dissect this change, so that they could make sense of it. Aristotle was able to map out this change in the human psyche, and reveal a changing relationship to the external world as it was happening. This is a marker of when we began to further personalise what previously belonged to the tribe. Our knowledge was in the form of an unconscious intuition where we had a 'feeling' for things. Each stage of soul development gave us more personal responsibility and a greater ability to think coupled with a renewed need to understand ourselves. Unconscious intuition is replaced by conscious thinking.

In this book we will look at the three discernable regions of our soul identified by Aristotle. We will see how they have slowly evolved over the last three thousand years and continue to do so. The first region of the soul—*Orektikon*—reached its peak around the time of Plato and Aristotle. These great philosophers heralded in the development of the second region of the soul—*Kinetikon*—when reason, logic and thinking became the focus of human life. When the responsibility for the soul was passed from the tribal elder to the individual person, he was also given responsibility for his actions. Not everyone took this responsibility seriously so at this time the legal system on which we depend today had its roots.

Individualism is associated with the human spirit

Examination of history and philosophy reveals that in the early Christian centuries while our reasoning/logic soul region was developing, we also started to develop an individual sense of self. The human being began to say "I" and mean himself as a separate being from his tribe or group. We began to speak on our own behalf and make individual choices. We developed an 'I'dentity. This "I" is the human spirit.

We are now working on two aspects of our developing consciousness.

The Renaissance marks the third turning point in the development of the soul, which has now teamed up with the spirit, the "I". At this time, a third region of soul—*Dianoetikon*—began to emerge which we can identify as awareness; or being conscious of our self (our spirit) and our intentions and actions in relation to our environment. This can be seen reflected in the paintings from that time—especially in the emphasis on the importance of portraying individual people.

While we develop our awareness by finely tuning the way our feeling, thinking and will work together, we are also working on our I-connection. Never before has the development of human consciousness been so intense. Never before has there been such diversity in human consciousness.

It is interesting to consider that when humanity didn't have full use of the soul and didn't have an awareness of his personal "I", the role of the Pharaoh and the King was important. The diminishing role of royalty (especially since wwi) all over the world is testimony to the development of the highest soul level, as well as the awareness of the human spirit through the strengthening of the sense of self. Perhaps the death of British Princess Diana in 1997 or the murder in 2001 of the Nepalese king and queen by their son, or the rejection of the authoritarian Nepalese king in 2006 has a message to tell. These are the kinds of things that we should think deeply about; they may be the signposts of changing consciousness.

The three regions of our soul

The essential operation of our three soul regions coincides with the three soul activities; feeling, thinking and willing. The way we *feel* can be referred to as our *impulses*, the way we *think* is found in our ability to *reason* and our *intentions* reveal the level of our *awareness*. We can therefore identify regions in the soul and call them impulse, reasoning and awareness regions. In our observation of ourselves, and others, we can observe that one or another soul region can dominate—or operate alone—for a period of time or in a moment of time. Some people feel a lot; some think a lot and some people are more aware and wiser in their actions and intentions than others.

These regions also develop as we mature. When we are young, our feeling dominates. As we grow older, thinking is added to feeling. Finally, all three regions work and (hopefully) we are wise! In many people one or other of these functions are automatic or unconscious. The aim is to express all the regions in a balanced, controlled and conscious way. The more mature our I-connection, the closer the goal.

In summary, their basic sphere of action identifies these three soul regions or soul qualities as the regions of:

1. *Impulse*: receiving an impulse; receiving the input of the senses, recording sensation.
2. *Reasoning*: logic; creating harmony in our thinking, resolving our ideas, intellect.
3. *Awareness*: becoming aware of all sides of a thing; having wisdom, measured intentions, being conscious.

The lower soul region is the most comfortable.

For the most part we live out of the impulse region of our soul. After all, we have been using it the longest. We are therefore dominated by the main force of this region—feeling. Because of this, we do not use the other two regions of reasoning and awareness as consciously as we could. Rather than rigorously thinking, it is human nature to develop formulas to reach conclusions automatically with as little effort as possible.

On the other hand, people who use their rational mind a lot operate primarily from the reasoning region of soul and often suppress their feelings. When we work exclusively from the rational mind we can have tunnel vision or blinkered vision. It is the balance between thinking and feeling that moves us into the highest soul region, the area of awareness, where we can see many sides of a situation with objectivity. Then we can consider all things out of which we act with the right intentions.

Having said this, we should avoid making abstract distinctions between our feelings, our thinking and our will (intentions) because they never operate alone.

It is the will element that links or separates our thoughts. Feeling always permeates our thinking when we decide to like or dislike something. We experience feeling in our will when we are satisfied or dissatisfied with something we have done. Also, will plays through our feelings to give life to our thinking. If we think of walking the dog, it is not until our intentions are fired up with the warmth of feeling for the love of the dog and its well being that our thought really comes to life. Otherwise it is just a thought and the dog won't have its walk.

Thinking and feeling are more conscious in our soul, but the more our feeling is involved with our will, the less conscious feeling is. Then we react to something instinctively without thinking. There are many other permutations which can be quite specific to us as individuals.

The soul forces interact with each other in different ways.

So it is important to understand and identify the many ways feeling, thinking and will work as a team, and that there is always a measure of one in the other. One can be the catalyst of the other. Thinking can be generated by either our feeling or our will or both, which means our motives can be unconscious, unbalanced and subjective. Feeling, especially in its intensity, can be mistaken for the will. This is often the case when a person is described as wilful. Their highly charged emotions masquerade as well thought out, and powerful, intentions. These soul faculties will be explored in more detail in chapter 3.

The ideal is to have all the regions and faculties interweave harmoniously, each one balancing the other, together with a strong I-connection. If we operate from one region more than the others – which can be habitual—it indicates that we are stuck in a rut. For example, if we habitually operate from our thinking we will be consistently unable to take in new impressions and will tend to rigidly defend our theories. Or, on the other hand, if we meet a new situation with our feelings when it really requires a great deal of thought—because we may not be able to muster the energy required to think the situation through—we may reject it on our feelings alone. There are many ways to see how we operate in a one-sided manner, by identifying how we gravitate to a particular region of the soul in our responses to life.

When we look at how the soul interacts with the world we can understand, from a different perspective, the functions of feeling, thinking and willing. Picture yourself looking out the window, or talking to a colleague at work. Impressions and events enter into us in this way:

1. Firstly, we take in the impressions through our bodily senses into the first soul region; in other words, we get an *impulse* from the outside world. We then have feelings about these impulses.
2. In the second soul region we make something of the impressions by thinking them through, by *reasoning*. We compare them with past impressions and make something of them.
3. In the third region we become *aware* of the fullness of the impression and make a decision to act or not. Here we can develop healthy intentions.

It is easy to see that we don't always follow this pattern. We can take in an impression and not think about it. We simply take it in and do nothing with it and we may say that something escaped our notice, but when questioned about it we do actually have the image of it in our soul. Another possibility is that we take the impulse in and think about it, turning it over in our mind but don't do anything about it. If this were to become habitual we become stagnant. We can even skip the middle soul region, taking in an impression and then act without thinking. Or, if we looked out the window because we heard a strange noise, it can take a while to work out what the noise was. These are some of the many possibilities that make up the activity of our soul.

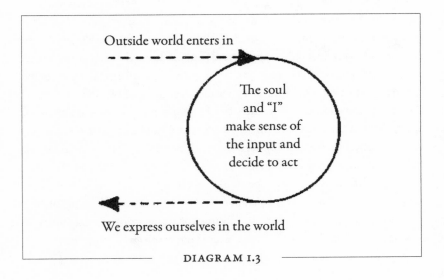

Outside world enters in

The soul and "I" make sense of the input and decide to act

We express ourselves in the world

DIAGRAM 1.3

When all three regions work in
a balanced way, our awareness is heightened.

When an impression moves through the three soul regions in a balanced way it finally reaches the third soul region where we form our intentions and hone our awareness. Then we are then able to act wisely in the world. How wisely depends on the involvement of our "I". These processes form the activity of our soul. It is a rhythmic breathing process; our soul inhales the impression, digests it and exhales as intentions.

By now a bigger picture of the nature of your own soul should be developing. You will have started to experience, in some way, how your unique soul activity defines who you are. You may have experienced how your soul talks to other people through shared images, a kind of soul-talk if you like. With this understanding, get ready to step into the next chapter and come to know your "I" in a deeper, clearer way. Before we do there is one other topic that should be clarified, if we are to have a clear understanding about the nature of the human soul and the human spirit.

The human being is not an advanced animal

How often do we hear experts say that the human being is an advanced animal? Some of the most respected academics say it. There can be no justification for saying that a human being is an advanced animal. We can say that the human being does sometimes express animal qualities. This can be described as "human-animal" behaviour, a human operating on the lowest level of humanity not the highest level of animality. We can also identify that animals act with more dignity than some human beings, which means that some human beings operate at a sub-human level. This can be the case when human beings take certain medication. For example, a mother describes her ten-year-old son on medication for Attention Deficit Disorder as "an empty shell with no soul." Addiction to narcotics fosters sub-human behaviour, crippling the soul and causing the human spirit to flee.

The right observation will reveal that we are not animals. Animals are a level of life below us, as plants are a level below animals; minerals are a level lower still. Animals can reveal aspects of the human being, but humans are superior to animals. Some plants, such as carnivorous plants, can reveal aspects of animals and some minerals, such as crystals, reveal plant-like qualities. However, each belongs to its own class.

Through our own observation of the world we can see these classes differ from each other. As children, when we played, "I spy with my little eye," we asked for a clue by saying: "Is it animal, vegetable or mineral?" Really we should add another class, human, and say, "Is it human, animal, vegetable or mineral?" Although young children may seem to be like animals in terms of basic needs and training, they do, however, contain a potential that does not exist for an animal. Higher animals, while they resemble human beings in some ways, remain animals.

Unlike animals, a human being has a highly developed memory and speech. It can be shown that this results from our blood flowing vertically in our body. Blood, as we will see in the next chapter, is associated with the "I". Unlike animals, we are also infused with the sense of self, the "I" which we call the human spirit. The scientists investigating a family in Turkey, in 2006, where some of the children "devolved" to walking on all fours, could have something to say about this when their research is published.

Another difference been humans and animals can be found in the drive to eat. Animals are driven to find food purely by their hunger, perhaps a reason why animals eat things human beings wouldn't dream of eating. The human drive to eat arises as much from the memory of the pleasure or satisfaction of eating as it does from the hunger. For example, the people whose nutritional requirements are met via a tube in hospital still want to eat. This difference relates directly to the human soul and spirit.

Consciousness differentiates man from animal.

A human being can also think; we have consciousness. Pavlov's experiments showed that an animal could be conditioned to repeat an action when it was linked to a stimulus. A conditioned response is not thinking. The ability to follow orders (for example, 'fetch') is not reasoning, but training. The ability of chimpanzees to dress themselves and sit at a table is not due to consciousness, but imitation. Thinking, reasoning and logic, as well as a highly developed memory, speech, dexterity and the ability to stand upright, set humans apart from animals.

We associate animals with instincts and these instincts can also be found in humans in certain circumstances. They arise out of the lowest levels of the physical body where we can find the basic levels of the human will. These basic will levels govern the forces of growth, nutrition, reproduction and restoration. In an extreme case, this force of will makes it possible for a mother to lift a car off her child in a traffic accident. Our instincts, drives and desires which originate deep in our physical body are expressed primitively unless they can be harmonised with the forces of our soul and spirit.

The animal behaviour which can manifest in a riot, or a crowd panicking, occurs because people do not use their own soul levels and they become a group-soul motivated by the prevailing emotion, usually anger or fear. We call them a mob because they lose their sense of individuality, their sense of self, along with their ability to reason and to refine their intentions.

The framework for all of these ideas will be explored though this book. Those who are already working with these ideas find the proof of them everywhere in life. They are not theories, nor do they introduce a jargon; but in simple everyday terms they have practical application in the most basic human expressions and interactions. The whole point is to become awake and aware of our true humanity.

As we identify the soul qualities of the human being we come to understand more fully how the human spirit, the "I" or "self", expresses itself in our soul. We are then able to observe that soul qualities vary from person to person, region to region and from age to age. If you find these ideas foreign, then continue; dip into the pages of this book and put some of the information to the test in your daily life. You can find the proof of these observations wherever you look in society.

Chapter 2: Human Self: the "I"

What is the "I"?

We know that each person is an individual with a specific character, a particular make-up, and each person expresses self in the world accordingly. This 'self' is the name we call ourselves when we say "I". The "I", the self, is the essence of the individual, it is our "I"dentity. Because it is an integral part of us, we often do not notice what it is, or how it works. The "I" is the kernel of our personality which we cannot grasp as we are not able to grasp our right hand with our right hand.

Our "I" enables us to function as beings of soul and spirit, not just as physical beings. Our "I" experiences the world through our soul and body; they are its vehicles. As we have been discussing, this is a developing thing, an evolutionary thing. Our "I" is not a fully conscious part of our being yet. Its connection with our body and soul grows over time; the more it grows, the more conscious we become. Then, the more we are able to have original thoughts and ideas, and also to be flexible about our thoughts and ideas. We could also say that meaning originates in the "I". For instance, when we speak, specifically about something we have thought about ourselves, the meaning from our "I" is expressed through the vocal cords of our body.

Our "I" can be found in our ability to concentrate, to be attentive by focussing our attention and by being observant. The more we can do this, the stronger our I-connection and the more conscious we are.

It is when the "I" shines its light into the body and soul that we become conscious. The light can shine brightly or dimly and fluctuate. If our "I" is only loosely connected to our soul this is because, in its natural state, our soul is in a dreamy sleep. Then our soul conducts our life through automatic responses of learned behaviour stored in our memory. We could call this the 'pseudo-self' which gives us a sense of "I", but as if in a mirror. When our I-connection is strong, our responses can be more spontaneous, and possibly more appropriate. Our task is twofold; to awaken our soul and to work on our I-connecting.

Consciousness of the "I" is evolving.

So while our relationship with our "I" is developing we can't view the "I" in its completeness. As mentioned in the previous chapter we have only had a personal connection with our "I" for less than 2,000 years. Prior to that, the Kings and Pharaohs fulfilled this role for us. Now that our relationship with our "I" is developing, we no longer need these external rulers. There are many other signs of this evolution towards personal responsibility for ourselves; for example, it is evident in the move from feudal law to democracy. It is also evident in the rejection of organised religion. We are in a tenuous phase at present as we assume this respon-sibility. This is the reason this book is written, so that more people will become aware of the possibilities that lie ahead.

We could describe our relationship with our "I" as a maturing process. We have to get used to connecting up with it as our soul is awakened. Some people refer to the "I" as the Real Self or true self, which it is in its purest expression. At the other end of the scale we can speak of our ego. Our ego could also be called our immature I-connection or the pseudo-self. The term 'ego', which is sometimes used to describe 'self', is a combination of the immature I-connection and the lower untamed or natural soul levels. Hence we speak of people being egotistical. The stronger our I-connection and the less dreamy our soul, the less egotistical we will be.

Experiencing the "I"

There are quite a few ways to experience the "I". One of the most powerful ways is to ask ourselves this question: "Who is thinking?" Or, if we are feeling unhappy, to ask, "Who is unhappy?" The only way we can recognise that we are unhappy is because not all of our being is unhappy. In our soul we experience the difference between happiness and unhappiness like a pendulum swinging. The soul can become polarised between happiness and unhappiness. It is the "I" that balances and harmonises these feelings in our soul and raises us up so that we can look on these feelings more objectively. Then, we can experience both happiness and unhappiness without get sucked into one or the other, or be pushed from one to the other. The "I" is the objective fulcrum which balances the polarities in the soul. We will look at this in more detail in chapter 5.

How dependent or independent are we?

The "I", as the essence of our being, is our individuality, our personality and it reveals itself in our independence. The soul, on the other hand, is that part of us that likes to depend on others for approval, or encourages others to depend on us. When our I-connection is mature we prefer to connect up with others as equals, we enjoy peer to peer co-operation.

The extent to which we can express our "I" depends on conditions in our soul and body. When we become aware of the difference between our "I" and our soul it becomes clear that the "I" can be expressed through our soul in varying ways; strongly or weakly, maturely or immaturely, and anywhere in between. The soul can indeed be a dark place if the light of the "I" cannot shine in. In this respect, the "I" is the hero, who works against the dark forces in our soul. It is not unusual for people to ask, "Where are the heroes in the world today?" The real answer is that the hero is now within us.

This paints a complex picture of the human being. The inclinations of the soul, and the influence of the "I", interacting with the body; each one can affect the other or be affected by them. When we become more aware of the interplay, our confidence is strengthened, and our self esteem is increased. A feeling of self-worth builds up in us and we no longer rely on others to show us how valuable we are. We accept ourselves in our uniqueness, and resist external pressure to be what someone else may want or expect us to be.

So far we have been calling the "I" the human spirit. It needs to be recognised that there is also another spiritual aspect to our being as shown in diagram 2.1, which is beyond the scope of this book. However, we mention it because those who understand the human being in its finer expression may wonder how this other spiritual aspect fits into the picture being presented here. While we refer to the "I" as the human spirit, strictly speaking the "I" is a separate thing from the higher spiritual aspect of our being. This higher spiritual aspect of our being becomes conscious when our "I" has a greater influence in our body. The "I" spiritualises our body and soul raising them from a lower, less conscious expression, to a highly developed and finely tuned consciousness.

The "I" in its highest expression is our Real Self.

In summary, the "I", from its highest expression in the Real Self, to its lowest expression in the ego is a continuum of consciousness covering the spectrum from super-conscious to unconscious. Our purpose is to express ourselves as consciously as possible through our "I" rather than unconsciously, habitually, through our unawakened soul and ego. This is an evolving process in humanity in general, and it also happens in each of us during our lifetime. When we understand that this is a work in progress, and that it happens in each of us differently, we change our expectation of our self and others.

Our relationship with our "I" develops over our lifetime

There are many ways to identify the way our "I" works in our life. Firstly, it is this "I" which leads us from birth to maturity, and it can be observed by the changes in our facial features during life. If we place, side by side, the photos of ourselves taken on our birthday each year we would recognise the influence of our "I" in the changes in our face. The facial expression of some people can change markedly at certain stages in their life; this usually indicates that their "I" has been able to exert itself more strongly in the soul. This sometimes happens through a life-changing event. The strength to navigate life's challenges comes from the "I". The letter "I" gives a sense of strength because it resembles a vertical iron rod.

When we are born we do not have a close connection with our "I". First our soul engages with our body at, or soon after, birth, as mentioned in chapter 1. This is when we see that the new born is able to focus their eyes. Later on, there is a point when the "I" is activated. This moment arrives when, as a child we begin to use the word "I", instead of our name, to refer to ourselves. At this moment, for the first time we say, "Yes, *I* am thirsty" or "No, *I* am not thirsty now" when previously we would have said: "Carol is not thirsty" or, "David wants a drink".

The "I" is responsible for our ability to stand upright, to speak and to think.

What happened for us to be able to say "I"? We started to say "I" at the point when our "I" began to connect up with us between the ages of about one-and-a-half to three-and-a-half. The sign that our "I" is connecting is when we develop the ability to walk, talk and finally to think. Before this time the expression of our "I" is under the guidance of our parents and carers, just as our body is kept for us in the womb of our mother until it is developed sufficiently for independent life.

> Emma-Jane Murphy, the Cellist, tells a story about when she was three-and-a-half years old. She was playing with her toys when, on the radio, she heard a Schubert Sonata. Her mother tells her that she stopped playing with her toys and sat very still, listening to every note of music. When it had finished her mother said, "That was such a beautiful sounding viola." Emma-Jane said, "No mummy, it was a cello." Her mother insisted it was a viola but the three-and-a-half year old just knew it was a cello. To this day Emma-Jane cannot explain how she knew this.

Our "I" is always associated with our talents, and in this story, the talent in the three-and-a-half year old was awoken at the moment she began to experience her own "I". It was through her connection with her "I" that she was able to respond to the music in the way she did. This is an example of the moment in life when a child becomes 'self' conscious.

The experience of the "I" comes to us as a strengthening, an uprightness (like the letter 'I') and a quiet confidence. One person explained her experience in this way, *"I have never forgotten that strange feeling that something tall and very old 'stood up' in me."*

The "I", as was said, is closely linked with our ability in early childhood to walk, talk and think and therefore is associated with our voice. We see further evidence of this in the breaking of the voice in male teenagers. There is also a connection to the development of the "I" when females menstruate.

The "I" reveals itself more fully in our late teens.

The "I" does not become fully independent in us until we are in our late teens. If we observe teenagers carefully we can identify when this takes place, usually between the years of seventeen to nineteen. At this time we often say that they have "come out of themselves". They begin to express their individual personality. Up until that time, the majority of teenagers tend to imitate the influences around them, while at the same time claiming to be individuals. This is evident in the way they must wear certain clothes, speak jargon and try to control what their parents wear, say, and do, if they must appear in public together.

Turning twenty-one is a significant time for our relationship with our "I", and indeed we can track our lives in seven year periods which we will discuss in the Appendix. In the third seven year period, we become more responsible, and we experience moments of self assurance which we haven't yet experienced in life so far.

> When I was in the interview for my present job there was a moment when I felt two feet taller and experienced a 'growing into myself'. I felt in control, and relaxed, at the same time. It was a moment of calm—not a sort of Hollywood-Nirvana sensation, but calm. I felt distanced from my emotions and physical condition. There was a sense of lightness, of having less earth gravity, yet I was balanced and more aware of what was happening in the room. [John aged 23]

We especially focus on the development of the "I" for the seven year period from twenty-one to twenty-eight. Many relationships formed earlier, break up around the age of twenty-eight. This is because of the changes associated with the "I" having more influence in our lives. The activity of the "I" continues to grow as we mature into adults. The degree of this maturity depends on the way life-experiences are dealt with. The maturation of the "I" is not a given, it depends on how we work on the I-connection. For the most part we act out of our soul, according to what we have learned. The automatic responses in our soul are learned in two ways; from the "I" at those times when it can connect up, and from our social environment.

Identifying the "I"

To assist the "I" to develop the strongest possible connection with the soul, we must first identify its activity. The "I" functions at the core of our soul, but it also interacts with our soul as if it is independent of our being. This means that the soul can act alone, or it can co-operate with the "I". The way to recognise these two different activities is to notice that the "I" is a more constant activity which expresses itself in the fluctuating soul life, to a greater or lesser extent.

The "I" is the captain of our soul.

The "I" is like the captain of a ship navigating the swell and the calm of the oceans. This picture gives us a sense of the constancy of the "I" and how it can connect with the movement of the soul. The soul has a similar unpredictability to the ocean; the "I" has the discipline of a ship's captain.

While we talk about these facets of our being; "I", soul, and body, keep remembering not to picture them as separate components; they are an interweaving activity. They can be pictured as swirling and inter-weaving colours which retain their own colour in places, and mix to form new colours in other places; all in continual motion according to the circumstances of life. See diagram 1.1.

Our personality, talents, wisdom, experiences, our dreams and goals —these are the characteristics of our 'self', our "I". It is natural for us to express ourselves out of our soul and, as we have seen, this expression can be unconscious and automatic. This, however, need not be the case. The awakened soul can be extremely conscious and in control.

Our "I" is revealed by the way we act in the world.

The difference between our "I" and our soul can be revealed in the things that we do in our life. In an interview, Paul McCartney pointed, perhaps unknowingly, to the full power of his "I". He said, *"This is just me in here. Paul McCartney is some guy over there doing amazing things. If I thought that was me constantly it would blow my head off."* This is a statement from a person who can compare the difference between expressing his talent to the maximum through his "I", and the way he is generally in everyday life expressing himself out of his soul. His experience was that he could not live with the intensity of his talent all the time. He was recognising that a lot of the time we sink into our soul levels and only fully express the potential of our "I" at certain times.

This brings us to a difference between "I" and 'me'. When we express ourselves though our "I" there is a selflessness about it. The 'me' in us is much more self-centred, introverted and egotistical. The more mature our connection with our "I", the less 'me' focused we are. Through our "I" we are more thoughtful and aware of others; we don't diminish ourselves for others, we stand in equality with others; we each have equal importance regardless of status. We are also able to stand within the other person and experience what they experience—to a greater or lesser extent.

Self consciousness separates us from the world.

Like the captain of the ship, our "I" directs our attention outwards into our environment. We see ourselves more connected with the whole outside world, while being separate from it. If the captain's attention was only on the ship and his crew, his vessel may hit an obstacle in the ocean. We meet many obstacles in life when we are self-centred or 'me-centric'. This is not to say that we should deny self for others in a martyr-like way, but that we should seek the balance between focus on self and our experience and thoughtfulness of others.

In many situations in life it is difficult to see the difference between our soul and our "I". Our awareness of what is soul, and what is self, is accentuated when we are conscious of the world around us. It may sound ridiculous to point out the obvious, but observation tells us that objects in the world are not part of us; we only have to stub our toe on a rock to know that. In fact, it is for this very reason that we are able to say "I". We are able to say "I" because we know that we are separate from the tree that we see; and when we see a tree, we are conscious of our self standing over against it. In the myths of ancient cultures there is a suggestion that, in our consciousness, this may not have always been the case.

To come to a closer understanding of this "I", we must become more conscious of the fact that we cannot say "I" and mean someone else. "I" is our own personal name. We refer to the other person as "you". This name, "I", refers to a specific personality which others can identify. Therefore, the way we express our "I" assists others to recognise us. If when we meet someone, and we don't remember much about them, it usually means that they are not expressing their "I" much at all. The importance of this point will become clearer as we progress.

Individual or group expression.

The essential nature of the "I", the self, is that it is very motivated to participate actively in life, to experience life, often in an independent way. The person who lacks this motivation may not have a strong connection to their "I" because they express themselves predominantly through their soul. They want to do what others are doing, rather than to individually express themselves; they are a follower not a leader. It should be noted here that many expressions of independence are motivated by our ego, our pseudo-self which acts out of an immature I-connection, for example, when we refuse to be helped by someone because we want to do things our own way rather than co-operatively. When individuality is emphasised in this way it is egotistical. In a social context, we come across some people who prefer to be part of a group expression while others dislike groups and prefer the individual expression. When we have a strong connection with our "I" we are individualistic while at the same time in harmony with the group.

A good test for how strongly our "I" expresses itself is to see how objective we can be; the more subjective we are, the more we are under the influence of our soul, or worse, our pseudo-self. In some situations, we can be very objective, but in others, our soul swamps us with emotion, and our reactions take over.

Compare how we express ourselves in our different roles throughout the day. For instance, at work, especially in leadership roles, where our talents are called upon, we would tend to express ourselves through our "I". During leadership, we deal with many situations which require us to be objective and productive. When we are in our home environment, we are often more relaxed and our soul levels bubble up, and we could say that we are off-guard. When something happens to disturb this relaxation, the lower soul regions can react because we haven't got the energy for a measured response. This does not mean that everyone operates through their "I" at work, and indeed, this is the place where ego can be rampant. These are just examples of the range of expressions we can have in one day.

The "I" can have too much influence.

It is definitely possible for the "I" to have too much influence; this presents a person with an isolated view and a lack of warmth towards others. This is quite a different expression from the one motivated by ego. It can be recognised by the amount of power behind it. The over-emphasised "I" is a trend in the world at the moment because of the evolutionary development of our soul and "I". There is a feeling of invincibility that accompanies the maturing I-connection. If it is not balanced by experiencing life from the other person's perspective, it can cause damage. Huge corporate fraud must surely be an example of this. The balance between ruthlessness and being overly sentimental must be struck.

> The Chief Financial Officer called me into his office late one afternoon. On his desk was an organisational model of all the State Managers. He was shifting them around like chess pieces. He advised me that for the company to achieve its budgets these managers would need to be relocated as soon as possible. All I could think about was the trauma this would cause the families; I knew that one Manager's son was doing his final exams and another was expecting a baby soon.

A sense of community can assist to maintain the balance, where priority is given to the well-being of the others in our group. One place we can see this sense of community arising is in self-help groups. One place we can see the isolation escalating is in the numbers of people living alone (it is now estimated that one in four people live alone), as well as the trend for people not to marry or form committed relationships. This is not necessarily a bad thing, it is part of the evolving I-connection, but it is important to ensure that sufficient contact is made with others socially.

> In the late 1980s, in my medical practice, I began seeing more and more young female executives who were depressed. Their companies were transferring them interstate, putting them in one bedroom flats, working them twelve hours a day, and they had no connection with fellow human

beings outside work. I began referring them to an agency to increase their social networks rather than prescribe medication.

While this can be seen as a symptom of modern society, it is also a sign of the development of human consciousness. We can seem trapped between the urge to be with others, and the inclination to be a separate individual. At the same time, it seems to get harder and harder to know the inner being of each other, however, the balance comes through the I-connection; and then, when we are alone, we will never feel lonely. Also, we won't isolate ourselves or allow others to isolate us. These are the areas where knowledge of the hidden aspects of our being can lead to greater understanding of social trends as well as health trends.

How the I-connection is a work in progress

As we have already discussed, we have evolved from the tribe to the individual, which means that our soul and spirit were not as intensely linked to the body as they are in human beings today. This also indicates that we have not had personal responsibility for our "I" for very long. We can trace its development within social cultures throughout history. By admitting that ancient humans could not understand today's science, is to point to a change in the constitution of our soul and its relationship with our "I".

Men and women of today have a much greater sense of self, of their "I", than even fifty years ago and the activity of the "I" continues to develop. The presence of Pharaohs, Kings and Queens in the world remind us of a time when people did not have to manage their own "I". The demise of royalty all over the world is a sign that we are now left to our own devices. We have to take responsibility for ourselves; we can no longer place this responsibility outside ourselves.

Historically, we are in a transition from a time when inner responsibility and individual freedom must replace the outer laws of government created to control the masses. No greater example of this can be found than in a global government policy called 'tittytainment' described as a mixture of deadening entertainment and adequate nourishment that will keep the world's frustrated population happy. The more governments create laws and policies to control us, the less we are likely to exercise self-responsibility. This weakens the "I" and encourages dependency on something outside ourselves. This means that the "I" is bypassed.

We need to experience how the developed "I" is self-regulating. Something deep within us knows that we are over-regulated by external rules and policies. We are moving forward to a time when more and more people are taking seriously the personal responsibility to consider what effect their actions will have on another, thus diminishing the need to be regulated by others. A strong I-connection fosters a powerful new conscience.

Observing the awakening forces of the "I" in us, and in others, has a strengthening effect in itself. The awareness of self and its boundaries is often revealed in our language: We can say that a person goes "beyond themselves", or "has little sense of themselves", or they may be "wasting themselves", or "not making the most of themselves". These phrases reveal that we innately understand the measure of the "I" that works in our being.

Different cultures have different soul moods.

By surveying people across the different cultures of the world, it is obvious that the "I" and the soul develop differently in the different countries and regions of the world. Consider Europe and compare and contrast the soul mood of the Spanish and Italians with the French, the British, the Germans and the Russians. Also consider the Australians, the Malaysians and Japanese, the Americans and the Chinese. This is backed up by the scientific research that cannot find genes associated with race. We can observe this development from many angles which are beyond the scope of this book.

Our developing connection with our "I" can also be linked to the emigration of people from their country of birth. However, multi-culturalism can counteract this by encouraging people of one culture to congregate together in their new country without integrating the customs of the new country into their lifestyle. This works against individuality. The very nature of the "I" is displayed in intermarriage between different religions and cultures. This breaks down barriers and changes the focus of being human to the individual rather than the group.

One of the most persuasive indicators of this developing "I" is the increasing number of single people in the world. People are marrying later, more than ever many are not marrying at all, more people have multiple marriages, and the average length of marriage in many regions of the western world is around seven years. This could also be connected with the seven year cycles listed in the appendix.

The developing "I" impacts on relationships.

The development of our "I" in a relationship can be difficult to manage because the maturity of the "I" fluctuates from person to person. We can get out of step with our partner and tensions arise, causing conflicts, which at times can be difficult to reconcile. Patience combined with understanding the experiences of the soul and the "I", can mean the difference between staying together or separating. Sometimes a challenge will come into the life of a couple which draws them closer together or separates them irreconcilably. This can often be traced directly to the soul-I connection.

The signs and stages of the developing "I"

In our quest to become more aware of the activity of our "I" and our soul we can respond to life in a variety of ways. While we can observe the I-connection developing at different rates in different people, we can also experience the I-connection fluctuating in our own being. There are four basic types of experiences to watch for and we can experience any or all of them throughout the day. Because we are all affected by others in our environment, the dynamics of our interrelationships can be the catalyst of any of the following experiences.

1. AN IMMATURE I-CONNECTION IS SELF-CENTRED.

Just as a baby has little strength, yet ensures its survival by focussing on meeting its needs, so too the immature I-connection of an adult reveals its lack of strength when a person is self-centred and demanding.

A weak "I" over-emphasises itself. The egotistical person who is self-absorbed, attention seeking and boastful often acts this way because they are just discovering the power of their "I" and do not yet use it wisely.

Nevertheless, such behaviour serves a purpose: it boosts the sense of "I", the sense of self. It is better for a person to experience their "I", their sense of self, than to not know or express it at all. This can be expressed as individuality that doesn't think of others. Hopefully it is a passing phase in our life rather than our continual *modus operandi*. There is a watch-point here; that our pseudo-self does not take over.

Hasty conclusions and pre-conceived ideas exclude the "I".

While the sense of self may allow us to proceed confidently, it only takes one of life's challenges to throw us back to our previous coping mechanisms. The strongest resolve in the world to engage the best possible connection to our "I" may not be effective in some situations. This is all part of the process and we should be accepting of self and others. One of the greatest qualities of a mature I-connection is that it withholds judgment until all things are considered. Jumping to quick conclusions, and being bound to pre-conceived ideas, counteract the development of our "I".

Another challenge for those with an immature I-connection is the rise of reality television shows. The maturation of our I-connection is threatened when it experiences life through the lives of others. We need real-life experiences of our "I" connecting up with our soul and shining its light there. Many areas of life, like reality TV, work against the I-connection. Of course, facing challenges always has a strengthening effect, however, do we deal with the situation by emulating what we saw on TV or do we use our own soul-resources? It is not a question here of being critical of television programmes, but of recognising what helps and what does not.

2. FEARFULNESS THAT OUR "I" IS THREATENED
MAKES US OVER-CONFIDENT OR WITHDRAWN.

At another stage, when we sense the growing connection of the "I" within us, we can become protective of it, fearful even, that we will lose this precious new possession, or that others will diminish it. Unfortunately, fear of losing our identity, our individuality and independence can distract us from strengthening our I-connection. Fear can lead us to either become over-confident, or withdrawn in our interactions. The result is that we either want to gloss over difficulties or not deal with them or even to crawl into our shell and ignore them. In other words, this protective measure does not protect the development of our "I"; it negates the "I". Fear stops us fully engaging in the world; and engaging with our immediate environment is essential to the maturing I-connection.

We can be confident that the I-connection will mature if we work with it. It is not uncommon, when our connection with our "I" is beginning to develop in us, to feel threatened by others who have a more developed relationship between their "I" and their soul. This can reveal itself in scoffing or trying to bring the other person down to our level. So, if we are being scoffed at it could be a sign that our I-connection is strengthening. With a more mature I-connection we do not retaliate, we are patient with others in their journey to mature their own I-connection.

3. A MATURE I-CONNECTION ENGAGES WITH DIFFICULTIES.

The key is to stand firm with the developing "I" energy and not be thrown to and fro in our defensiveness or fear. Once we recognise this growing energy of the "I" in our soul we can attempt to recreate it in times when we are thrown off balance. This skill will take time to develop, and we should not be discouraged when we forget, when caught off-guard. Engaging confidently in the world enhances the normal development of our I-connection. We need not withdraw from, or leap over, difficulties, but can instead meet them objectively.

Engaging with difficulties does not mean a struggle.

We can engage with the resistance placed in our way as a kite must meet with resistance before it can fly. It does not mean we struggle with difficulties but that we acknowledge the difficulties, and accept them or deal with them as objectively as possible. This may mean that we walk around them. This also means that we do not hold expectations of our self that are too high. These episodes in our life are character building; they strengthen our I-connection and make our soul more active. The activity in our soul is generated by having to think new thoughts, by changing the way we feel about things and acting differently.

We can see from these descriptions that a pendulum swings from one extreme to the other. This is important; registering the full spectrum of experience as we work with our I-connection enlivens us. We must keep the pendulum swinging widely for if it does not swing we stagnate; it is through our "I" that we can regulate this.

4. A STRONG I-CONNECTION CAN LOOK BEYOND SELF.

When we have a strong I-connection we have the ability to concentrate our attention on a single thing at will. Usually our attention is only focussed when there is a personal need or a duty. This ability to focus our attention assists us to look beyond ourselves. We don't just focus on our body, turning our attention inwards; we can direct our attention in endless ways and feel ourselves to part of the world; part of everything and everyone in it. Also, we don't focus our attention rigidly on one thing; we have the ability to change the focus of our attention leaving ourselves open to new possibilities. When we are able to concentrate in this way we become aware of our real self, we are REAL-"I"-sed!

There is nothing more important in our life than to strive to enhance the way our "I" and our soul work together. We work to strengthen that connection so that we become as conscious as possible. When we have an agile soul which accepts the influence of our "I" we can relate to the "I" of another person harmoniously, respectfully and thoughtfully. We can give them our undivided attention. We also don't allow others to impose their will on us. This maturing I-connection is like the ship's captain navigating his ship smoothly over the ocean.

"I" is for individuality and independence

Our individuality, our independence, our uniqueness, our personality; these are the ways we express ourselves in the world. Remember that within the "I" is where our talents lie. Whether we are a good cook, an artist, a wise person, a practical person, a humorous person—all these qualities are part of our "I". Whether we are outgoing or withdrawn depends on the calibre of our I-connection within our soul; we interact with circumstances and people to the extent that our personality allows.

True individuality is not self-absorbed.

The development of the "I" also brings with it problems, for the motto of the "I" is freedom and with that comes independence. The expression of individuality can be quite divisive at times. When we experience our "I" strongly we can make strong statements. We can dare to say things that usually would not be said. In this situation the other person is likely to respond by saying, "You are welcome to your view, I see it another way." While this seems to express individuality, and display a good nature in allowing you your point of view, it actually creates a gulf between you. True individuality does not encourage opposing views; it considers and observes many views in panorama, which gives a more complete view of the situation. We can never have a complete view of a tree by viewing it from just one side.

While we explore the I-connection, realising that the possibility of connecting with our "I" evolves over time, we can see that not everyone is at the same stage of connecting. We can also see how people connect differently. As previously mentioned, the connection with our "I" can be expressed in lower or higher ways. When it comes to freedom, we need to be able to recognise the two extremes because they can occur within minutes of each other.

I. WHEN FREEDOM IS EXPRESSED AT THE LOWER LEVEL, WE CANNOT THINK BEYOND SELF.

When we only think of expressing our own free will, our actions can lack consideration for others, for example, throwing litter in the street or leaving the dog's poo where others will walk; or perhaps something more dangerous, such as ignoring the road rules when we drive the car. These are times when we cannot put ourselves in the other person's place because our own sense of self is weak. It would feel like we were not guarding home base. If we have a genuine experience of our soul and "I" we experience our immediate environment as part of ourselves.

I was walking along a busy shopping strip and outside a public building was a little oasis with trees and seats for shoppers to rest. One young fellow was picking the bits that he didn't like out of his salad sandwich and dropping them on the footpath. Later on when I returned by there, he had gone, but his discarded salad remained on the footpath.

While this man experienced the freedom to act as he pleased, he was only thinking of himself. True freedom has an innate sense of responsibility and a consideration for the well-being of others. Freedom is not about our own convenience. That is very short term thinking.

2. WHEN FREEDOM IS EXPRESSED ON A HIGHER LEVEL, THERE IS UNITY WITH OTHERS.

When we experience another person as if they were part of ourselves, we will treat others as we like to be treated. This is neither the charity of being a do-gooder, nor the duty of self-sacrifice. This is a genuine feeling of community in which we feel what the other person feels, as if we were them; their joy is our joy, their sorrow is our sorrow. Most of us are far from experiencing this, or only experience it with our family and close friends. Between these two extremes are many valuable experiences which contribute to a greater connection with, and consciousness of, our "I".

How conscious are we?

We are only as independent and individual as we are conscious of our self and others.

This consciousness of self is not what is meant in common usage by "self-conscious" (where it generally refers to a form of awkward shyness). True consciousness of self is an entirely different matter. How conscious are we of how we act in the world? How conscious are we of others when we act?

> The pressure is always on in a restaurant where I work. The kitchen staff are always performing at a premium. I was concentrating on the preliminary preparation of the main courses and trusting that everyone was meeting their own responsibilities. I suddenly became aware of one of the junior chefs on the other side of the kitchen; she was very quiet and subdued. No one else seemed to notice, they were so absorbed in their work. I took over a cup of tea and suggested we have a quick break and she told me that her cat had been run over last night and while the vet was hopeful she was anxiously waiting to see for herself after work. I couldn't understand why the people who work around her all the time had not noticed her distress.

The spectrum of individuality ranges from:

1. Having no thought for others, being self-absorbed, arrogant and static.

2. Struggling to be unique while working with others.

3. Being able to be unique while blending with others. Such individuality is continually developing, mobile, and expressed *in the world.*

All three may be operating in us at different times during the day. The crucial point is that we develop our powers of observation. If we increase our awareness of our self and others, we can get better at recognising which level is at work and this awareness gives our "I" a greater chance of having more influence in our soul more often.

There are many exercises that we can do to be more conscious, they are not difficult and produce good results quite quickly. These results are also self perpetuating. See the exercises in chapter 5.

Signs of the "I" at work in our lives

The quality of our I-connection can be measured by how objective we can be. The world enters into us in various ways, not always as we plan. If we become more aware of how this happens, we can be more prepared, and acting objectively comes more easily. Take a moment to picture again how the outside world enters into us as discussed in chapter 1. Impressions or impulses approach our soul through the senses in our body. In broad terms it is a rhythmic process as shown in diagram 1.3.

This is the same model as our respiration; breathing in, holding, and breathing out. With regards to our soul, an event occurs outside us, it enters into us through our senses, we feel something about it, we think it over and then we apply our wisdom to it, which leads to an action, or a decision not to act, depending on our level of awareness.

The more our "I" is strongly engaged in this process the more objectively we will act, the more consciously we will respond (rather than unconsciously reacting to the event), and the more thoughtful we will be.

Think about shopping at the supermarket. The person behind you has one carton of milk and you have done the weekly shopping. If you let them go ahead of you, their experience is entirely different to the way it would be if you didn't let them go ahead of you. If you are the person with the carton of milk, and the one who has done the weekly shopping does not invite you to go through the checkout before them, can you remain objective and not be overwhelmed thinking of their thoughtlessness?

Whether one person is more aware and observant than another depends on the strength of the I-connection; the more aware a person is, the greater the connection. Observe people at the supermarket, they are very often in an unconscious reverie.

I-Connecting can cause anxiety.

Another observation that can be made is that the developing I-connection presses down upon our being trying to enter more fully into our soul. As we work with the "I" we may experience this pressure as a sense of inner urgency or generalised anxiety. We may experience the force of the "I" as an intrusive threat, as a feeling that something is taking us over. However, as we become more familiar with our "I" we will understand that this is a natural experience as our "I" establishes itself in our soul; it is finding its legs and claiming its place in the team.

We can respond to the pressure of the incoming "I" in a higher and a lower way:

1. THE CONSTRUCTIVE RESPONSE to the "I" shows itself when we trust, when we love, when we are open, encouraging, patient, thoughtful and when we forgive. These processes build up the I-connection.
2. THE DESTRUCTIVE RESPONSE to the "I" is experienced in fear, paranoia, insecurity, negativity, the need to be controlling, feeling overwhelmed, expressing bravado and feeling isolated. These forces work against the I-connection.

If we are honest, we feel all of these things at some point daily in our lives. It is part of being real with our self to do so. We are then in a position to recognise that the positive and negative sides of the swinging pendulum of our experiences are in the process of creating a balance.

The pressure of the "I" can be released through addictions.

Some people try to release the pressure that can accompany the I-connection through the use of alcohol and drugs and other escape mechanisms like gambling and computer games. The "I" can have nothing to do with something that reduces consciousness. This explains the feeling of impotence and loss associated with addictions.

Many of the issues that arise in our culture point to the teething pains of the I-connection. Governments spend millions on research which hardly scratches the surface of the issue. It would be more useful if they would observe the cause and encourage people to explore and manage the underlying symptoms. Education about gambling will not prevent gambling. Education about the emerging I-connection will reduce the inclination to addictive behaviour.

How the "I" interacts with other people

It is helpful to build a more complete picture of what happens when we interact with others. The following may sound like a science fiction script, however, if we observe ourselves carefully we will be able to confirm that what will now be described does indeed take place. When one person meets another, when one "I" meets another "I", this is what happens— remember that our soul and our "I" are like a cloud around us and within us that mingles with everything that is in our immediate environment.

With our "I" we enter into others.

When our "I" encounters something or someone outside itself, our "I" has to penetrate into the nature of the other person or thing, in order to grasp it. So when we meet another person, our "I" has to enter into them. We do know this because we talk about 'entering into a thing' as a measure of how involved we are with it. In order for this penetration to occur our "I" must surrender its own opinions, knowledge, understanding, etc. We can't enter into the other person with our own baggage.

Once we have entered into the other person, our "I" takes a copy of what it experiences there and then compares it with the contents of our own being. We then decide whether it pleases or displeases us. Can we understand it or not? Is it similar to some of the things we have in ourselves or is it very different? If it is different, we have to decide if we can assimilate this difference? The following situation explains how this can happen.

As a favour for a friend I once agreed to let Usha (an Indian woman whom I didn't know) stay at my house for a couple of days while she looked for other accommodation. On the first night I was going to arrive home late. I asked Usha whether she would mind cooking dinner and told her I had put out a recipe and some vegetables. I tried to make some connection at this point. I felt it didn't happen, so I decided to sort it out when I got home. When I got home, dinner was ready and I thanked her very much. She was very stiff in her response and I could tell I had in some way offended her but couldn't guess what it was. I continued to flow out towards her in warm comments about the food, saying I couldn't believe the same recipe could taste so different!

Finally, I felt some barrier loosen inside her and she began to speak about why she was offended: She told me that in India, to give someone a recipe is to imply they have not had a mother to raise them! When she saw the shock in my face she knew that was not what I had intended. I then told her that I had only been trying to be helpful because when I was busy I found it a chore to think of a recipe and wouldn't want to look around another person's kitchen to work out what to do. It took quite a lot of effort on both our parts to reach this point of understanding. We were culturally foreign to each other and it was difficult to overcome such difference. I understand more about the feelings I was having now. The barrier was not some underlying racial problem, but a real encounter with differences as we tried to enter into each other.

Our "I" constantly tries to bring itself into harmony with what it took back into itself from the other person. If what is outside warms us, we form a bond, we connect with it. These experiences that come to us are reflected in our soul life and influence our physical body. Here lies the key to why we often don't understand the other person; we are not prepared to set aside the contents of our own being to enter into the other person. Therefore we can't bring the picture of them back into our own being. So how can we ever know them?

Occasionally in our life we encounter a person and feel that they know us completely. It could be a teacher or an employer who we implicitly trust. What has happened here? Such a person is able to make us feel like this because they have such control of their "I" they can enter into us, experience us totally, come back into their self and speak back to us as if they *were* us.

Avoid getting lost in other people.

This should not be confused with the love experienced in intimate relationships which makes us more willing to enter another person. We can be 'lost' in the other person during the first flush of enthusiasm in a relationship. Here the "I" of both people can be renounced. This can be quite enjoyable as it relieves the pressure we feel from assimilating our "I".

Every time we are totally focussed on ourselves, or we want to talk only about ourselves, then we cannot know the other person. We can't possibly enter into them; we are too occupied with ourselves.

Our "I" expresses itself in our body, specifically in our blood. There is a direct connection here to when we blush, for example. Such responses assist us to identify exactly how our body, soul and "I" respond to our environment and the people we meet. Our "I"

◇ stirs our emotions;

◇ corrects the currents in our body and in our memory; and,

◇ affects the blood flow in our body (for example, in fright we pale, in embarrassment we blush).

Once we have dropped all our baggage and we have entered into the other person, and have collected our information, then we experience a response in our blood. We may feel a range of emotions—from love to embarrassment, to fear or anger. This connection to the blood is also reflected in our language, for example, we may say, "They made my blood boil."

Be patient as the I-connection develops.

We do not always enter fully into another person. Sometimes this is to do with the stage of development of our "I". For example, as mentioned earlier, if our I-connection is newly awakened, we may not feel confident to enter into the other person; we may fear being swallowed up by them. Or, if our I-connection is tenuous, we may be reluctant to give up our position to enter into the other person. However, another possibility is that we are capable of entering in, but do not do so, because we feel a sense of danger as we begin to enter into someone we would term 'bad'. We are able to judge that the state of this soul is totally incompatible. In this regard, we also speak of "blood curdling experiences".

Our inability to enter into others can be overcome through our strengthened I-connection. Certainly there may be times when we feel strong enough to enter into a situation and other times when we just don't have the strength for it. However, what is important is that we continually strive to strengthen our I-connection and enter into others as much as possible. It is not just the action of entering into others, but it is our actual striving that strengthens the connection between our "I" and our soul.

Our "I" feels especially in tune with our environment when it finally understands something through self-effort. We cannot feel good about entering into the other person and then coming back into ourselves, unless we strive to understand what we encountered there. Striving is not soul-friendly. Many people are reluctant to leave their small circle of friends and family because they cannot make the effort to experience different types of people. Prejudice and intolerance can result from the lack of effort to enter into others outside our immediate circle. The "I" will have nothing to do with prejudice and intolerance.

Scorn or defensiveness point to the budding I-connection.

We must continually try to observe the ways in which we relate to different types of people, because this will assist us to understand how our I-connection is developing. If we can't allow ourselves to enter into the other person to the full extent then the relationship cannot be a close one. If our "I" cannot surrender its own force of knowledge and understanding, it isn't possible to enter into another person or thing. When we are faced with this challenge we can sometimes laugh with relief or cry with frustration. Both laughter and scorn indicate an unwillingness to enter into people or things outside ourselves. As we saw earlier, scoffing at a person often indicates an immature I-connection which is protecting its own forces against the presence of a more highly developed "I".

A person with a growing awareness of their "I" can also be quite protective and defensive in the presence of someone with a stronger "I"—they fear that they will have their own budding I-connection taken away by the stronger person. Only through trust in the strength of our own I-connection can we gain confidence. While the "I" innately has a sense of depending on self, in a world where the "I" is evolving, and people are at various levels of development, we can often be faced with the decision to dive into the other person and trust that our "I" will prevail, rather than retreat to our soul's comfort levels.

It can be more difficult to develop the "I" when in a relationship.

It can be a challenge to maintain our sense of individual self in relationships. Our feeling of being swallowed up in the "I" of the other is valid because that is exactly what happens. Nevertheless, we can experience the 'swallowing up' without losing our own sense of self or behaving defensively. As stated earlier, living alone can strengthen our "I". This is one of the reasons so many people are not in partnered relationships today because they must develop their own I-connection and stand strong in it. However, living alone can also mean that we are escaping the natural development of the "I". So sometimes we need to alternate between the two. Consider these statistics again: over 30% of people are never going to marry, and many partnered relationships last on average no more than 7 years. Many people have several committed relationships throughout their life because when we have awakened our "I" to a certain point we need to find others who have developed their "I" to a similar or higher level.

The "I" affects the parent-child dynamic.

Parenting is another area of consideration. A mother can cease to operate through her own "I" levels when her child is born. For a while, she and the child share their "I" expression, and both must wrestle to gain control of their own "I" when the time is right. Parents and carers are the custodians of the soul and "I" of the child until the child is ready to take charge of them. As previously mentioned, it is not until the late teens that we start to fully integrate the "I", and this can be observed in the changes to posture and development of facial features at this time. Teenagers see themselves as individuals but this is an expression of their graduation from childhood, not a sign that the "I" is integrated. Observing teenagers is an excellent way to understand the pseudo "I" or pseudo-self. The pseudo "I" defines itself externally, so is unable to be an individual that stands confidently alone. Among teenagers this shows in their desire to wear certain clothes, use certain words according to the fashions of the group to which they belong.

Adults will sometimes forfeit their individuality by allowing another person to dominate them, for example, in a relationship when one partner is subservient to the other. Or when a person lives their life through another person; this can happen in a marriage or in a family. A parent who devotes themselves to their child who excels at sport, for instance, will sometimes admit that they are making up for their own lack of success in that area. All of this is tied to the development of our I-connection or lack of it.

How can we assist the "I" to connect?

The "I", like a musician, can play the notes of its soul-instrument in any order—creating harmony or discord. Through both harmony and discord, the soul becomes a flexible tool in the world, with a broad repertoire to deal with all the different situations that arise. Discord may resolve into a new harmony and our soul will sing a new tune. Mistakes are simply a learning mechanism. Discord, disharmony and pain can assist us to strengthen our I-connection; yet we are often discouraged to enter into them.

The outside world enters into us, we think, feel and act accordingly.

As we work towards developing a stronger I-connection, the essential thing is to *experience* fully what happens as we move around in the world. From the moment we get up in the morning the outside world enters into us. We hear sounds, smell the toast, and feel good to see our family or our pet. If we haven't slept well, we still feel tired, if we have slept well, we feel invigorated. All this information is being processed in our soul. We take the information from our senses into us and notice the state of our body. We think about what time it is, how long it will be before we begin work, and what we have to do between now and then. So many things enter into us, stimulating our soul—and this is just as we wake up! Then we act. We get out of bed; we have a shower, get dressed, and eat our breakfast. This input/output system can be observed in everything we do in life. (See diagram 1.3).

What is happening in this process? What are we taking in, what are we doing with it when it is within us, and how are we putting it out? How is this supposed to work and what happens when it doesn't? There are three possibilities:

1. WHEN WE TAKE IMPRESSIONS IN FROM THE OUTSIDE AND DO NOTHING WITH THEM, our "I" is not active within our soul.

Some people take impressions in from their environment and keep them within them, and do nothing with them. This is a form of inertia, the "I" is not active and has little influence in the person's life; it is not working with their soul, nor is it acting on the environment, making a contribution.

Inertia is the enemy of our soul and our "I".

Like a stone when it is pushed, such a person's life just keeps on rolling, that is, until it hits an obstacle. There may appear to be movement, but this movement is accidental since there is no conscious, directing action involved. Inertia has set in.

Using this example; if we take something in, and do not integrate it into our life, then we are just rolling along, picking up whatever lies in our path. Our soul operates in automatic ways. If we decide to work with the impressions we encounter, if we actively apply the information we receive, this indicates that our soul is active and our "I" is engaged. This is not so much about how we acted, but that we acted at all.

People with this inclination to inertia often agree to do things and don't carry it through. They can talk very enthusiastically about doing a task but their attention is continually distracted by the next possibility that comes their way.

2. WHEN WE TAKE IMPRESSIONS IN FROM THE OUTSIDE, CON-SIDER THEM, AND ACT UPON THEM, our "I" is not only productive within our soul, but creates the world we live in.

Some people take impressions in from the outside world, actively work with them, consider them, and then purposefully act on them. In a rhythmic way they move back out into the world with purpose, they affect and change the world. They are putting their stamp on the world by creating something that was not there before they acted. Here the "I" is productive and active in the world.

*An active "I" gives us the boldness to act
imperfectly and the courage to learn from mistakes.*

We encounter an active "I" within a person who is prepared to 'have a go', even when they know that their resources may not be adequate. These people experience more and learn more. Unfortunately, social pressure often gives us the message that it is best not to act unless we can act perfectly. This imprisons and negates the "I". We are discouraged from acting, and through this, we miss out on experiencing things and growing. It is helpful to change our attitude about making mistakes when we are striving for a stronger I-connection. It is certainly better to have tried than never to have tried at all.

If our I-connection is strong then our "yes" will be yes and our "no" will be no. We will meet the commitments that we make to others and to ourselves. We will be willing to enter into uncertain situations. We will be prepared to discuss difficult issues and engage in enough conversations to be able to work out resolutions. The person whose I-connection is strong always wants things to move forward, to explore new possibilities.

3. WHEN WE TAKE IMPRESSIONS IN FROM THE OUTSIDE, SOMETIMES WE CAN ONLY DREAM ABOUT ACTING ON THEM.

Illness can assist with the I-connection.

Some other people dream of acting in a certain way but are unable to do it. Others dream of doing a certain thing and never even try to do it. Then, when such a person is faced with a life threatening illness, or has a brush with death, they will do this thing which they have dreamed of doing for years. In this way we can see that illness can prompt a stronger I-connection.

So far we have been building up ideas of the presence and purpose of the "I" in our own being. We have also looked at how the I-connection is an evolutionary phenomenon. These ideas can be traced through the events of world history and also through the history of the consciousness of mankind. Now we can consider what lies behind the need for us to connect our "I" and our soul.

The purpose of developing our "I"

What is the purpose of developing our I-connection? Why have we evolved from a tribal or group consciousness to an individual consciousness? Is it for purely personal benefit or does it benefit the world also?

The work we do on ourselves to strengthen our I-connection is not just solely for our own benefit because it enables us to contribute to the way society is formed. Cultural progress is closely tied to the way the connection between the soul and the "I" develop in each human being. We each contribute to this progress by the way in which we personally awaken our soul and allow our "I" to shine its light there.

Those who do not work on their I-connection are self-centred and cannot think of how their actions affect others. They are unconscious of how they are creating the world. They are also the ones most likely to complain about the way the world is.

How our actions change the world does not just apply to the individual; it applies equally to the decision-makers in business. How many large companies made commercial decisions in the past without consideration of the effect for the future, for example, the use of asbestos in construction or lead in paint and petrol? The policies of these corporations are developed by individuals. Therefore the degree to which their policies do not consider the well being of the human race is the degree to which the policy makers have not worked on their own I-connection. This situation continues as we are now faced with new issues such as global warming, cloning, nuclear waste disposal and genetically modified crops. The difference in the way these issues are dealt with can be directly related to the maturation of the "I" of the individual who contributes to policies within business and within government.

The danger of bypassing the "I".

While we can readily see examples of the evolving "I" there is much evidence to reveal the tendency in the world to bypass the "I" and to see the soul as our real 'self'—especially the lower expressions of soul. This is what is meant when social commentators say "we are only herd animals after all." Such a statement denigrates the "I" and undermines the dignity of the human being. These commentators are actually referring to what Aristotle called our animal soul which is a level below the human soul.

When we are led to form ideas about human-animal behaviour there is an inclination of governments to over-regulate which weakens rather than strengthens the I-connection. We strengthen the connection to our "I" the more we are able to make moral judgments using our conscience. These are the signs of the mature I-connection.

The world is changed by each person's actions. We create the world.

There are many examples that show the difference between a person who acts on life and the person who moves through life without much deliberation. When we become aware of the difference, the importance of our action in the world is revealed.

Considering these issues we can see that we *are* responsible for the world and we change the world whether we are conscious of it or not. The following simple picture shows how we have the ability to change the world in every day life: a branch from a tree is hanging over the garden path. We can either remove the branch by pruning it, or we can accidentally bump into it and break it off—perhaps even being injured in the process. Pruning, the act that is undertaken consciously and purposefully, is obviously more timely and harmonious.

Of course, a timely and harmonious act is more complex when it involves other people. It often requires the persistence of a consciously held aim within self, as well as an experimental creativity in responding to others. For example:

> An office worker decided to make the unattractive entrance to her office look better with an arrangement of large pot plants. Those entering the next day were pleased with her efforts. However, when she left the office that evening she was distressed and disappointed to see that several

people had put their discarded chewing gum in the new pots. Both actions: her beautifying arrangement and their thoughtless littering created the environment at the end of the day. She could have remained angry, but instead she found another way to achieve her aim—by placing a bowl of sand nearby for the gum.

A person who has awareness always
looks for a solution that suits both parties.

There is no point arguing with a person who isn't aware of the environment or who does not respond to beauty. Such a person is cocooned within their soul. The vital signs of their soul are failing; they neither take in the world, nor flow out from their soul to express themselves in the world. Their connection with their "I" is unconscious. See diagram 1.3. They are only aware of their own convenience—by default not by design. They view the environment in terms of what it provides them and they view others in terms of their usefulness to them.

> I noticed when the water restrictions were first imposed that many people still used their hose to remove leaves from verandas and driveways instead of sweeping them away. It took quite some time for them to be more thoughtful about the use of water.

This insular behaviour points to the lack of community being experienced in the world today. Many factors have been named as contributing to this lack of connection between people, but at its heart, the problem is to do with the I-connection. A sense of community can sometimes seem to threaten the independence of the "I". However, as we become more conscious we will see how we each contribute to the well being of the whole community through our individual actions.

A new idea of community

In fact, many people are gradually forming a new idea of community where independence and individuality are respected and where the "I" is understood and encouraged.

Our aim is to work as individuals in a community of individuals.

To be an individual among individuals requires a different attitude to life than the one we have grown up with. It is a new endeavour. It is quite different from the old way of the tribe where harmony resulted from people being the same and following a leader. Today we are moving towards a community where family ties are not so strong, and where we are not even related to each other by the same blood. In such communities we allow people to be different and we respect the differences. Obviously a new and different sense of community arises from this. The peace and harmony of this type of community is not created through imposing external rules or rituals but rises up from within each person because as the I-connection grows in strength we assume more responsibility for self.

The type of harmony that is possible in a community of individuals is not necessarily one of agreement with another's ideas or actions. However, there is a commitment to working with any resistance encountered in the differences so that all the members of the community strengthen their "I". The key to this is to suspend judgment and resist forming opinions about others. The longer we can stay open to many possibilities the more embracing we are of any differences. Through our "I" we always seek to assimilate differences rather than discard them.

All the ideas in this book have been tested in many different ways by the author over many years. It is a wonderful thing to experience that once we are able to distinguish between our "I" and our soul, and see how they work together or against each other, we continue to see the evidence of this continually in our daily life. Everything we do assists us to build our understanding and continue our I-connecting.

"I" signposts

Our "I" is experienced in our response to life.

◊ The "I" is that part of us that can stand and not be rocked by a harsh or angry word. Every time we are rocked by criticism or the anger of another, our "I" is excluded. However, we are not perfect yet. I-connecting is a process and when we encounter criticism and unpleasant behaviour from others we learn more about ourselves. As we work to include our "I" we can increasingly respond in a more measured way.

◇ The "I" doesn't speak a harsh or angry word. When two people with a developing I-connection meet they delight in the strength of the other. If there is inequality between the I-connection of the people, it is usually the weaker "I" that will want to unsettle the other by saying something to 'bring them down to size'—their size. The challenge is for the one with the stronger I-connection to appear to be at the level of the one with the weaker I-connection. This always has an elevating effect on any situation. We hear it said that if you want to improve your game of tennis or golf, for instance, play with someone who is a little better than you are.

◇ The person with a strong I-connection knows their abilities; what they can and can't do. A person with a strong I-connection is also humble without being self-effacing. Knowing the limits of our abilities is important. Then we can confidently say that we *can* do a thing without embarrassment. If people call this egotism – let them! Conversely, if we *can't* do a thing, we should also say so without embarrassment.

◇ A person who has no boundaries, a person who acts with no regard for others, is not I-connecting. The "I" knows its boundaries and acts accordingly and with wisdom.

More signposts of the "I" can be observed if we watch the news and current affairs closely. The development of human consciousness can be observed in a myriad of ways in global events. The struggle for independence and democracy in nations like Timor, Iraq and Afghanistan is an example.

Turkish children reverted to walking on all fours.

As briefly mentioned earlier, in 2006 it was revealed that in Turkey some of the children in a family walk on all fours. When we consider that there is a link between the "I" and our ability to stand erect, this is a most intriguing event.

There must surely be implications for these people in Turkey who have not been able to stand upright to walk on their feet but instead move around using their hands and their feet. The scientists examining this phenomenon specifically noted that they use the heels of their hands not their knuckles as apes do. Rather than comparing these human beings to animals, they spoke of this as a sign of the devolving of the human being. Could this be the consequence of ignoring the importance of connecting up with our "I"? These things must be deeply contemplated as we explore the I-connection.

How does the "I" experience our soul life?

Now that we have explored the "I" in greater detail, it is important to look more closely at the relationship between the "I" and the soul. The soul has a much more natural connection with us than the "I", but while our soul remains sleepy we cannot become conscious of our "I" and connect up with it. Keep reminding yourself that these are not separate systems, they work together and their sum total makes the person that we are.

We have already looked at some of the issues of the soul-I connection, but before we move on to the look more closely at the soul faculties (feeling, thinking and willing), it will be helpful to build on our picture of the how the "I" experiences our soul life.

It is the "I" that experiences things in our body and soul.

When we consider that it is the "I", this unique human spirit, that does the feeling, thinking and acting through our soul, we realise that the stronger the I-connection, the more conscious our feeling, thinking and action will be. Remember that we have three regions in our soul where we receive *impulses*, where we *reason* and where we become *aware*. It is the "I" or 'self', or as Plato called it, the Genius, that does the experiencing. The German scientist, philosopher and artist Goethe puts it another way: "Vainly we try to describe the character of a man; but if we bring together his actions, his deeds, then his character will emerge from them."

In the following diagram we unfortunately have to depict the forces within us as separate parts, but in reality they are not, they flow into each other continually as we respond to life. If we can give our "I" a specific position then we must agree that the "I" is outside us and its point of contact is the reasoning region of our soul. The "I" is most conscious for us in our thinking.

The soul can eclipse the "I", like the moon eclipses the sun.

When the I-connection is loose we express ourselves egotistically. For our ego is to be found in our unconscious soul life. The more our "I" can engage with our being the less egotistical we are. This difference between the soul and the "I" can be elusive and they can become superimposed so that the soul eclipses the "I" altogether. If we are to experience the reality of our being we must become aware that the soul in its native state can be untamed and it is through the presence of the "I" that the soul can be guided and directed to greater consciousness.

The diagram below sets out the aspects of the human being as body, soul and spirit. The body has three forces or expressions; the physical flesh and bones, the drives and the desires. These are necessary to keep our body alive and make it a fitting vehicle for the soul and the "I".

Closely connected to our body we find our soul, and the region of our soul closest to our body is the impulse region.

While in this book we have been referring to the "I" as our human spirit, we also have a spiritual expression which is higher than our soul. This is beyond the scope of this book because this part of our spirit is in embryo for many of us.

Using the analogy of the "I" as the captain of our soul, the captain gives commands to the crew according to the impressions (*impulses*) that come to him through his senses, as well as through his calculations (*reasoning*) and through his wise experience (*awareness*), so that the ship will move through the water in the intended way.

Using this same analogy; if we feel hungry, it is the *body* telling the "I" that it is hungry, as the instruments on the ship tell the captain to refuel. This information can also come via the crew (soul regions) in a variety of ways.

When we appreciate beauty, it is the "I" that has a feeling response within our soul to what is viewed. The captain on the bridge may alert his crew to a beautiful sunset and they all enjoy it together in their own way.

While the captain and his crew are a highly tuned team, this is often not the situation in our own being. As we have described, the human being is evolving from stages of being less conscious to becoming more and more aware and conscious. We experience the proof of this daily

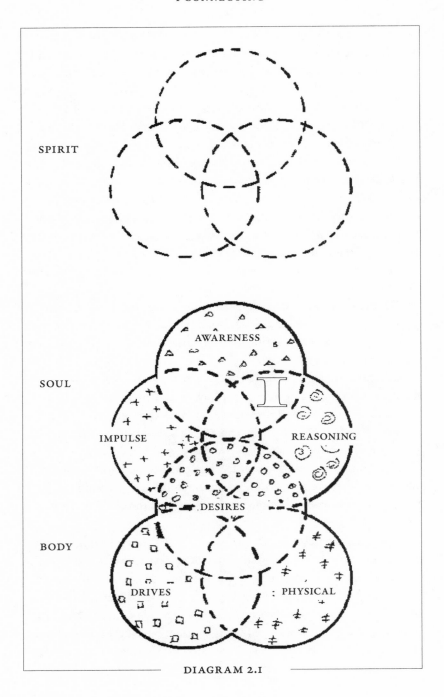

SPIRIT

SOUL

BODY

DIAGRAM 2.1

when we use technology for example. While we have used the first two regions of our soul for some hundreds of years, we are at present learning how to use the third region while at the same time gaining more and more control of the way our "I" interrelates with our soul.

We can ensnare the "I" in our soul so that it loses its mobility.

Our task is always to try to respond to our environment in higher, more refined ways. Feelings, emotions, natural urges, desires and actions prompted either by anger or love are personal for each of us. We unfold our personality through these expressions. When we become entangled in these things our "I" is not free, but it is ensnared and submerged in these life-events. We come to know ourselves when we become aware of the point of consciousness in our "I" from which we are able to observe these things without becoming entangled. This is the kind of objectivity we strive for. We can reach this by asking the questions: who is angry? Who is loving? Who wants to respond?

While laughter and crying are the essential expressions of our soul, our "I" is neutral in the combination of, or resolution of, the laughter or tears. To be able to shed a tear without wailing loudly and to be able to laugh without being raucous means that we are expressing ourselves objectively and with dignity. Then we can experience a blend of sorrow and joy.

The electron theory is a good picture of I-soul relationship.

The balance that our "I" can bring about in the soul can be explained using the electron theory. Diagram 2.2 shows how the three soul regions relate to our "I". Each circle or path represents one soul region. Each circle overlaps with the others and is 'excited' by the activity of "I".

The constant motion of the atom is a good model to show the continually active energy and balancing that occurs within the soul.

How our soul interacts with the "I"

While the relationship of our soul and our "I" is interactive it is not mechanistic. The "I" excites the soul regions to the extent that it is able. The cloudlike soul can connect with "I" in various ways. The "I" continually tries to enter into the right connection with our soul by using our feeling, thinking and willing. It seeks to harmonise these soul functions. The way we express these functions depends on our I-connection. Our soul's response is directly related to the degree of awareness we have. It is the "I" that deepens and harmonises our feelings, orders our thought images and refines and directs our desires. We can say that the "I" spiritualises our soul. We each do this in an individual way, there can be no formula. The quality of the connection depends on whether we can get our ego, our automatic pseudo-self, out of the way.

Not only do we each have a different relationship with our "I" but our soul experiences the "I" differently in each of its regions. We can summarise this relationship by saying that the "I":

◇ is a brooding presence in the *impulse* soul region.

◇ gains clarity in the *rational* soul region; and,

◇ becomes fully awake and conscious in the *awareness* soul region.

Teamwork is required between our body, soul and "I".

Keep remembering that to understand all these different areas we need to separate the components but it is important to view our soul, our "I" and our body as an integrated team. The picture of our soul as a three stringed instrument and the "I" as the musician playing it, is very helpful. The music created can be harmonious or disharmonious as we discussed before.

If what we create is not harmonious, it takes strength and courage to take the responsibility for it and to not blame someone or something

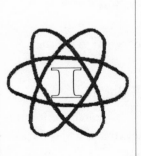

The paths of the three electrons circling the nucleus represent the three soul qualities. The nucleus, which excites the electrons, is usually the "I".

The conditions in the nucleus will affect the movement of the electron—its path being the oblique line. The behaviour of the electrons will affect each other, which in turn will have an effect on our environment

DIAGRAM 2.2

outside us. When we take responsibility for what we have created, it is a sign that we have a good working relationship between "I" and soul.

Using the analogy of the ship's captain again; our soul and "I" work together like a crew works with the captain of a ship. All is harmony and smooth sailing if the "I" is in charge. However, if our soul's forces act on their own, without following the lead of the "I", confusion, disharmony and even catastrophe can result. Then we can say that our soul has mutinied.

The "I" can act independently of our soul.

There is a further possibility where the "I" can act independently of the soul. If our "I" is not able to engage with our soul and tries to act on its own, our personality can become quite cool and distant and we do not engage fully in life. Just as the captain charts a course for the crew to follow, the "I" must signal its intentions to our soul. The "I" cannot be effective without interaction with our soul, without team support. An "I" that only engages part of the forces of our soul will steer the ship in circles. For example, when we act selfishly it indicates that the "I" is only working in the lowest, *impulse* soul region. If the "I" had a balanced influence in the soul then out of the middle soul region, it would *reason* and say, "Hey, you're not the only person in this world!"

When our "I" expresses itself in the highest soul region there is an intense wish for others to have what we have. We want to share possessions, thoughts, understandings, yet this may be annoying to those who want to develop things for themselves. We can liken this to a parent-child dynamic— the child insists on learning by its own mistakes, while the parent wants to teach ways of avoiding difficulty in life.

Awareness of our "I" strengthens its relationship with the soul.

The more we work with our I-connection, the more often we are conscious of it. In other words, our "I" becomes conscious of itself and the power of that awareness maximises our efforts. There is a synergistic effect. When we develop inner strength, our "I" is given room to tame our soul and create harmony and balance. The strengthened I-connection gains a momentum. We can become 'self-propelled'!

How the "I" works with the different regions of our soul

As we become more conscious of the interaction between our soul and our "I" we will notice that the activity of our soul is often drawn to our body's desires rather than to the higher regions of the soul and "I".

The strength of our I-connection is
revealed in our responses and reactions.

When confronted by something that we have to struggle to make sense of, our ability to deal with it is directly linked to the strength of our I-connection in the moment.

1. If our emotions swamp us so that we don't deal with a situation calmly and harmoniously, it means that our "I" has little or no say at the moment the impulse is received.

2. If we deal with the situation rationally it means that our emotions have been controlled and our "I", through our intellect, can direct a response and assist us to deal with situations reasonably. However, if we don't involve the first soul region it can mean that we deny our feelings. It can also mean that we don't have a sense for what is right or wrong.

3. Whether we deal with the situation wisely or not depends on the highest part of our soul, the awareness region. When this happens, our "I" and our awareness soul region work as a team and we make wise and conscientious decisions.

We all have examples of these responses. There are times when in great shock, we have dealt with a situation coolly and calmly. There are times when we have been angry at, or hurt by, something directed at us, and yet been able to make a wise decision. However, there are also times when our emotions have taken control, when we have been unable to make a decision or to restore order to our mind. Despite repeatedly asking for the advice of friends, we have continued to swim around in the myriads of possibilities.

My friend was telling me that somebody she knew carried out a disagreement and break-up of their friendship via text messages. Using modern technology in this way by-passes our "I". People do not have to look at the other person and see the consequences of their words; they escape any real interaction.

We experience the difference when a strong, solid sense of the "I" has been able to influence the situation. Yet just knowing how well the "I" has connected in certain situations does not mean we will be able to use it in every situation. There are many different elements in a situation that call out the power of the "I".

I was walking down the corridor when I heard a commotion in one of the patient's rooms. An old man was threatening to attack a nurse. I walked into the room and said, "Stop that and come with me!" The old man immediately did what was commanded and I directed him back to his bed.

Here the "I", revealing its authority through the voice, took control of the situation and the danger dissipated. In this instance, it was the threat of danger to another which called upon the power of the "I" in the person passing by. The experience may well have shaken the person but they were able to connect up with their "I" and show leadership in the moment.

A person may act promptly on witnessing a car accident where people are injured or even dead. The strength of their "I" takes charge. However, later, when their "I" moves into the background, the feelings from their soul and the drives from their body rise up, overwhelming their "I" which retreats, and the person experiences delayed shock. This is a normal response.

Those who work among the sick and disadvantaged face these situations daily and they deal with them compassionately and practically. How do they do this consistently? Their purpose and role in life has enabled their "I" to have a greater influence in this area of their life over the active forces in their being. Their I-connection matures and thrives on this experience. It does not necessarily follow that they apply this in all areas of their life or in all moments of their life.

If our relationship with our "I" is unconscious we operate in an automatic way. The more conscious of our "I" we become, the more conscious our feeling, thinking and willing are and the more conscious we are of our soul.

With these concepts in mind we can now explore the faculties or our soul, feeling, thinking and willing, in more detail.

Chapter 3: Three Soul Faculties: feeling, thinking, willing

The functions of feeling, thinking and willing live in our soul. They are our soul faculties which act as forces within our being. Our "I" works into our feeling, thinking and willing using them as its tools—to a greater or lesser extent. The stronger our I-connection, the greater we can control these forces. They can act automatically out of habit, or they can be consciously directed in response to the situations we meet in life. Like the garden without a gardener can grow wild, but if properly tended the garden can be a place of order and beauty.

Keep remembering that our being is not a combination of separate parts but one activity which moves and weaves to form the integrated whole person that we are. Our hand, for example, only operates as a hand while it is an integral part of our body—the severed hand is less useful than a table or chair. Even though we can examine the components separately, they function as an interactive set of forces; each one affecting the other in various ways. By becoming aware of these interactions we can alter them to assist our personal growth. We will now look in more detail at this activity.

Feeling, thinking and willing are the tools of the "I".

As we have previously stressed, the components of our being can be seen as a cloud or a mist of forces moving within and around our physical body. The focal point of the three regions of our soul can be found in the faculties we call our feeling, our thinking and our action. It is our "I" that does the feeling, thinking and willing. The stronger our I-connection, the more it can shine through these processes, making them more conscious and less automatic. Then we become increasingly aware of what is within us and around us.

It is like driving a car down a foggy road; the headlights of the car shine through the mist to illuminate everything. The strength of the light depends on the liveliness of our soul. This image demonstrates how our "I" works through our body and soul, using the faculties of feeling, thinking and willing to the extent that it can connect with our soul. There are moments when the lights shine brightly, the "I" has put them on high beam, and we see more than the fog that surrounds us. We have a wider view, one that places us in relation to the world. The "I" is driving the car (our body) and through the headlights (our soul) it can have a wider view. The reflected light assists us to see within the car as well. Take a moment to create this image in your mind and experience the interaction between your body, soul and "I".

Feeling, thinking and willing in the three different soul regions

By understanding how our feeling, thinking and willing work, greater insight into our soul is possible. Always bear in mind that feeling, thinking and willing are not independent forces; they work in concert, one takes the lead role, the others take supportive roles depending on the situation.

Feeling is experienced in the first soul region and it is the oldest faculty in human experience. The next faculty we developed was thinking. We are currently working on the awareness soul region and developing our will. In chapter 4 we will explore these soul regions in more detail; but first we need to have a good understanding of the force that is produced in our being and in our immediate environment when we feel, think and form intentions.

In a nutshell, this is how these three faculties work: We experience our thoughts in our head, our heart feels how alive or lifeless the thought is, and our will engages our "I" so that our thoughts can motivate us to act. The following story is a good example of the choices we can make in our soul in response to the events in our environment.

I took my children to ride their bikes at the local school. They were riding around the netball court when the gardener came along with his blower to blow the leaves away. He saw us and we said hello, but he was obviously very intent on his task. He came right up next to me and turned the blower on so that the leaves and dirt went all over me and into my face. It would have been useless to say anything with the noise of blower anyway, but I looked up at him, without anger, just to say, "Hey, I am here". Later as we were leaving we had to pass by him again, this time he was more aware of us and turned his blower off as we approached and waited as we walked by.

We act according to the calibre of our I-connection. This action should not be confused with an action that is an instinct. Action from our "I" is measured and founded on the harmony between thinking and feeling. If the thought is alive and the feeling is warm we are always considerate of others in situations like that described in the example above. If our action results in harming someone it is unlikely that we have thoughtfully monitored our feelings. If we retaliate when someone upsets us, it is a reflex action which is usually associated with the lower levels of our being where instincts are strong and the I-connection is weak. This is where we can act in a human-animal way. The quality of our actions is a direct result of the health of our soul which influences the way these soul faculties interact.

By placing feeling, thinking and willing into three interlocking circles we get an idea of the many possible ways the three processes can work together.

The teamwork of the faculties.

While one faculty takes prominence, the other two provide the foundation on which it can stand.

1. When we think; willing and feeling work underneath to support and warm our thinking.
2. When we feel; thinking and willing moderate and guide our feeling.
3. When we act; feeling and thinking assist our actions to be appropriate using care and consideration.

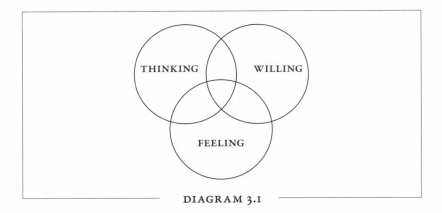

DIAGRAM 3.1

If these faculties act without the support of the others they create unbalanced forces in our being which can affect our inner strength and even our health. By becoming more aware of how these three faculties work together we can strengthen and regulate the connections. The more balanced our being, the easier it is for the "I" to connect.

By tracking the play of these three soul faculties in our being we will know how active they are and which one is dominant at any given time. This is an example of how it can happen. Imagine our boss asks us to take on a new task. We will probably say to ourselves: "I have to think about this". Our lowest (first/impulse) soul region has received the impulse (new task) via our senses, in this case our ears. We become aware of how we feel about it; if we like or dislike the idea. Then we respond by bringing our thinking (second/reasoning soul region) into play; we think of all the reasons it will be a good thing, or a bad thing, to do. While we are thinking, the feeling levels drop back a bit. After a while feeling will rise again to give us a 'feeling' for the 'right or wrong' decision. Our feeling is a barometer while also adding warmth to our thinking. At this point we can say to ourselves: "OK, I've made a decision and I know what to do. Now I can act." When we reach this stage we are operating through the highest (third/awareness) region of our soul and if wisdom prevails, all three regions of the soul are working together as a team.

Thoughtful action results from good teamwork.

Thoughtful action always means that we are functioning out of the awareness soul region with balanced faculties. However, the other possibility is that we might get to the second soul region and think: "Oh I don't know what to do" and we don't act. Or we may not even think about it at all and immediately say 'yes' or 'no'—this response comes from the first soul region, for better or worse (see further on in this chapter: 'The rhythmic process in the soul regions and soul faculties' for more on this).

As we become more conscious of the interplay of these faculties in ourselves we can observe how we take something in, think about it and make a decision. We will recognise certain patterns that have developed within us over the years and we will see how we can change these patterns to get better results. It is not difficult to detect the faculties moving around: feeling, thinking and willing each have a different 'quality'. Although, not necessarily the same quality in each of us, which is what makes us unique beings. The quality is directly linked to the I-connection.

These faculties are experienced in the soul, expressed in the body

Our body is the vehicle, our soul is the engine and our "I" is the driver.

When we say that feeling, thinking and willing are soul faculties, remember that while they originate in the soul they are expressed in the body. It is our body that carries the expression into the world; the soul is the engine and mechanical components, and the "I" is the driver. The quality of the driving depends on the maturity of our I-connection.

This is the picture that has been built so far: The threefold soul and the threefold faculties of the soul (feeling, thinking and willing) are expressed in our threefold body; its head, torso and limbs.

Placing this into our physical being a pattern emerges:

1. Thinking/intellect/ideas - HEAD
Using the nervous system and brain.
2. Feeling/senses, perceptions, wonder - HEART
Using the rhythmic system; circulation and breathing.

DIAGRAM 3.2

3. Action/will, intentions, ideals – HANDS and FEET
Using the metabolic system (digestion) and limbs (movement)

This creates a more detailed picture of how the "I" can use feeling, thinking and willing expressing them through our body. By looking more closely at these three soul faculties we see that they are not as straightforward as they appear. The body, soul and spirit work together and if a part of our being is not functioning as it should its effects can be felt in unexpected ways. We may ask that if something is physically wrong with our heart, would our feelings be affected? Certainly if we experience fear, our breathing is also affected and we go pale because our blood drains out of our face. Science may want to explain this from a purely physical point of view, however, it can be equally well explained using knowledge of the soul and "I".

What is thinking?

Develop intelligence in our thinking.

Thinking is a series of images that we have gathered in memory. Thinking forms ideas and it is through our ability to think that we have the capacity to form more mental pictures. By using our will we link the mental pictures together giving us the possibility of a wise understanding of the world. The quality of our thinking depends on the amount of effort we put into it. It is helpful to experience thinking as a living force. It is only through our thought pictures that we can experience a true representation of all that is within us and around us.

Thinking occurs in the second soul region, the reasoning region. The brain is the physical vehicle for the soul's thinking, but also the soul connects itself with our nervous system when it thinks, when it forms our mental images.

At this stage in our evolution, our thinking does not have as much life as it could have; its images are often old duplicates rather than originals. When the "I" streams into our thoughts it brings the images to life and we can see more clearly; like the strength of the headlights assists us to see through the fog.

It is interesting to note that thinking is universal, it transcends language; for example, the thought image 'tree' is shared across all borders. So, the one thing human beings have in common is thoughts, where we differ is in our language and soul mood. The more our "I" can stream into our thoughts the more we are connected with the whole of humanity, beyond culture or creed.

We can test the quality of our thinking by asking ourselves if we are reflective or not. When people are not thoughtful, it is not usually a sign of the lack of intelligence; it often points to laziness. We do not engage with the images that enter us through our senses; we just let them flow by, one after the other, like a movie.

If we do engage with the images, do we make an effort to continue our thoughts to the final end (by calling our will into action), or do we get distracted so that our thoughts are only partly formed? Worse than that, do we use the ready made thoughts of others as the basis for our reasoning, especially the thoughts that we collect from the media? Unless we put energy into our thinking our thoughts can be disjointed, second hand and not fully formed.

Concentration transforms thinking.

It requires a lot of effort to take our thoughts to the final end, to keep thinking about something until the thought is as fully formed as possible.

The modern world is so full of ready-made thoughts vying for our attention that our ability to think has been affected. If we do not put energy into our thinking our soul forces will be weakened by these outside influences. Purposeful thinking sets up a balance between thinking and willing, as if a pendulum swings between them; each one modifying the other. It is helpful to realise that the only way we can transform thinking is through concentration. Chapter five has exercises to assist us to develop our concentration.

What is the relationship between our ability to think and our intellect? Some scientists agree that most healthy human beings have a similar intellectual capacity. It is our ability to use our soul's faculties, and the degree to which our "I" is engaged, that produces intelligence in our thinking. The groundwork for this is developed in our childhood.

It is important to become more aware of our thinking. When we take notice of our thoughts we can be amazed at how many thoughts flow through our mind which we are hardly conscious of. It is surprising how often we think thoughts which are destructive—to us and to others. When we learn to observe our thoughts we can experience an expansion in our thinking process; one thought grows out of the last thought and so on. The more aware we are of this, the more likely we are to follow our thoughts through to the end. We are also more likely to arrest the destructive thoughts and replace them with more useful thoughts. When this happens we experience the power and potential of our human spirit in our soul.

What is feeling?

Develop sound and healthy feelings.

Feeling essentially recognises right from wrong. After we have thought about something our feeling rises up to say, "yes" I accept that or "no" I reject it. Feeling is the force of like or dislike, attraction or repulsion, joy and pain, warmth or cold. We also use feeling to recognise justice. Feeling and judging are connected because a positive feeling gives the soul confidence to move out into the world and act, whereas a negative feeling causes the soul to withdraw.

Feeling is linked to the rhythmic systems in our body, our breathing and the circulation of blood. So when we feel something, our breathing changes and our blood flow can be affected. This explains why we associate feeling with our heart.

Feeling is the prime quality of the first soul region and as such is the interface between the world and our soul. So feeling therefore is tied to the sensations that enter us through our bodily senses. In this way we either:

◇ just exist in the world as a physical body; or,
◇ experience the world within our soul.

We come to the real quality of feeling when we experience the tension between what is external to our soul and what is internal to it. When we look at a rose and experience the feeling of appreciation, the rose outside us stands over against the feeling inside us. In this way we become more aware of our self and our inner life.

Feeling is actually experienced as inner life because it gives life to our inner experiences. Think about the different expressions of feeling we experience in our friends and family. Some people don't seem to feel much and we may even describe them as not having much life in them. This happens when inner experiences are dull. Our feelings can be brought to life by purposefully appreciating, for instance, the beauty of nature or a piece of music.

Feeling is also a thermometer; are we in a good mood or a bad mood, happy or sad? When the "I" works through our feelings they are more tempered and we are more respectful because we appreciate the value in things and events—good or bad. Through a strong I-connection our feelings are more dignified rather than raw and primal.

Feelings can be guided rather than changed.

When compared to thinking, feeling is a more passive and receptive force. The feeling levels in our soul are dreamy, semi-conscious. In fact we spend a lot of our time resting in this soul faculty. It is helpful to realise that we cannot change our feelings through our own initiative; we can only guide them. It is like the dykes in Holland that control the level of water; sometimes they hold the water back, sometimes they let more water flow, but it is the same water, the water is not changed. So we can guide our feelings from sad to happy using our thinking and our will.

Because feeling is the faculty in the lowest (first) soul region closest to our body, and this is the level of the soul that we have worked through for the longest period of time, feeling is therefore the primary soul experience. As thinking is associated with our spirit, willing is associated with our body, so feeling is associated with our soul. This means that feeling can be an automatic expression which takes over our whole soul, if our soul is not awake and our I-connection is weak.

What is willing?

Develop strength of will.

Will is the force that enables us to take hold of life effectively and vigorously. We apply will to an idea to bring about an action in the world. It is the force that directs us one way or another. Will can also be identified as that impulse of warmth which develops into motivation; the will to do a thing. It rises up as an inner initiative. It is responsible for the movement of the physical body, our work, our independence, and the urge to activity, our volition and our intentions. Are we full of intent or lethargic?

Our soul connects with our metabolism and our movement when it is engaged in willing. So when we will something our hands and feet are often involved. Will is associated with third soul region of awareness and consciousness. When the "I" works into our will then our will can burst forth into our soul life and wake us up. Therefore we will become more conscious of our soul the more we develop the third level of our soul.

Meditation transforms willing.

Willing is expressive, in contrast to feeling which is passive and receptive. We can strengthen our will with our thinking, for example, through meditating on an object like a pencil, which is explained in chapter 4. We can transform willing through meditation. Another good exercise, which can make our will more conscious, is to review our day backwards as described in chapter 5. There are other exercises in chapter 5 to assist us to energise and harmonise the soul faculties so that we can use them more consciously.

The ways feeling, thinking and willing work together

For a balanced life, our feeling, thinking and willing must work in harmony, with one of the faculties coming to the fore as required and the others working in the background as a sustaining force. When we think without the sustaining power of feeling and willing, for example, then our thinking is unbalanced and often goes round in circles. Many psychological problems can be understood as an imbalance of soul faculties and a lack of I-connection. When one force is properly sustained by the others, these faculties become the real tool of the "I".

The sixteenth century philosopher, Descartes said, "I think therefore I am". Now that we have computers that can replicate thinking to a degree, perhaps we can rephrase Descartes. The fullness of the human being is expressed by saying, "I think, I feel and I will, therefore I am." In other words, therefore I am expressing myself out of the fullness of my "I". Perhaps Descartes was not able to understand the "I" as fully as we are able to do today; he lived in the period of time when the second soul region was fully developed and the third region of awareness was just beginning to stir.

We need clear thinking, warm feelings and energetic will impulses.

Our ideal is to have a close relationship between clear thinking, warm feelings and energetic will. See chapter 4, which describes in detail the three soul regions, for a more detailed description of the inter-relationship of these faculties.

As we develop our understanding of how these faculties work in our soul it is helpful to realise that in their natural state:

◊ our unconscious levels are found in our will;

◊ our semi-conscious levels can be found in feelings; and,

◊ we are only conscious, awake and alert in our thinking.

This is obvious when we look at diagram 3.3 showing the lifecycle of our soul. Thinking, because it is our most conscious faculty, is the master faculty of our being. It transforms feelings, strengthens will, and creates a rational coherence. We are able to use our thinking more easily than we can use our feelings or our will.

On closer examination we will notice that our thinking determines our feelings, and can transform them. Our feelings can run away with themselves if we don't use the dyke-like control of them by our thinking. If we are about to let the feelings from a bad experience flow through us, we can equally let thinking enter in and say: No, we are not going there now, we are going to think about this differently. We can replace the thought with different thoughts if we want to. What stops this being denial of our feelings is that the new train of thought can be again checked by feeling. Feeling in this sense has an active role as the mediator because feeling is always the moderator telling us if the thought right or wrong. Thinking and feeling must always act as a team; if they act alone we will usually experience difficulties.

The faculties of feeling, thinking and willing are active forces swirling around and through us, continually interacting with each other. The relationships can be seen in this way: Thinking gravitates to what is pleasing and what pleases us is found in our feeling levels. Then it is feeling that arouses the will. As previously mentioned, we should be aware that sometimes feeling is mistaken for will.

Thinking alone is abstract.

All of these processes work differently in each region of the soul and differently within each of us. The more we observe the processes and the forces they create, the greater understanding we will have of how they work in ourselves and in others. Feelings are more on the surface in the lowest soul region, the impulse region. They become more inward in the reasoning soul. Thinking alone is abstract; it must seize hold of feeling and will. Our thoughts are healthy when they are imbued with warm and enthusiastic feelings. If we notice that we are thinking a lot but this thinking leads us nowhere, we can stop and ask ourselves how we 'feel' about the subject of our thoughts. The action of stopping requires the will. We may then be alert to other will forces rising up as we move towards a resolution and an action.

Will is the foundation of our being.

From another angle, we can say that the foundation of our being rests on the will forces; in this respect will forces are even more important than thinking. We must work at developing a picture of the continual motion of our soul-life; the forces created by feeling, thinking and willing interweaving according to our experiences in life. Our soul life may at times move quickly, at times more slowly; this motion is caused by our will. One of the reasons we are more sluggish after we have eaten is because the will, which is associated with metabolism, is busy digesting our food. In other words, there is less will at our disposal.

I had been thinking for some time of getting more fit as well as working on the flexibility of my body. I decided that swimming would be the most efficient way of doing this, but putting it into action was another matter. I could see the need for my thoughts, feelings and will to work together. I found that thinking of fitness and flexibility, then feeling inspired and connected to what swimming would do for me, moved me more easily into taking the action. Originally, I had tried moving from thinking to action which felt like a lead weight holding me back in an old place.

If we stimulate our will then our thoughts and feelings flow more quickly. When our will is sluggish our thoughts and feelings amble along. The will is the prime mover that enlarges our soul life. So in this respect, first our will gives rise to our intentions, and then feelings and thoughts interact, followed by our will rising again so that we can act. All this lives and weaves within the life of our soul. See again diagram 3.3

Outer impressions meet feeling, thinking and willing

When we observe something in our immediate environment and the impressions enter into us until we reach the point of owning this new impression. The action of owning the new impression requires the motivation of our will. There are different ways to order the soul faculties, so before we continue it is important to have a clear picture of the two different perspectives of our soul that are used in this book:

1. upper and lower regions—feeling, thinking, will; and,
2. inner and outer experiences—will, feeling, thinking.

Till now we have been talking about the upper and lower regions, now we will look at things from the inner and outer perspective. Diagram 3.3 below uses the inner and outer view. So when we say that the act of owning an impression initially involves the will, this mustn't be confused with the fact that feeling belongs to the first region of the soul.

It is critical to make the distinction between the higher and lower regions of the soul and the faculties of feeling, thinking, will. In the *soul regions* feeling is the most elementary force, in the *faculties of the "I"* will is the primary tool. At the same time, *thinking* is the most conscious. Will is also the foundation of our physical body involved in metabolism and digestion. Thinking is the fundamental faculty of the *spiritual* part of our being. Simultaneously, feeling, thinking and willing are faculties at work in the soul. It may assist if you draw your own diagrams of these things so that you can develop a firsthand understanding of how they work in your own being. To become more conscious of these aspects of ourselves is simply a matter of keen observation followed by deep consideration of what we have observed.

How aware are we?

To take ownership of an outside impression that is passing through our soul requires the motivation of our will. How often do we walk past something and not notice it? Through the activity of the second soul region (our reasoning) we combine new impressions with our memorised images. If we notice the beautiful rose as we walk past it, we compare it with the memory of other roses we have seen. It is from these impressions that become part of us throughout our life, that the "I" builds up talents, in this case, the talent to judge a good rose when we see one. Notice that when a small child learns the name 'dog' they then call every animal they see, "dog".

So our talents are increased according the involvement of our "I". To the extent this happens depends on how much thinking is at work in our will. This takes place in the highest soul region where we experience higher degrees of awareness. This region of the soul is the home of the will and we must be mindful that will operating alone is not a good thing—to act without thought is always unwise as is acting without feeling. The meditation of focusing on a pencil, described in chapter 4, strengthens our ability to use our will when we think.

From these descriptions we can see how feeling, thinking and willing have specific roles to play in our being. These are but some examples. By becoming more aware of the roles these faculties play, and the forces they create in our being, we can sharpen our ability to observe the effect of using them in different situations.

When images and impressions from the outside world enter us through our senses they should then move through each region of our soul. During this process, if we infuse our thinking with feeling we can only do so in the second, reasoning soul region. In the first soul region, feeling is always dominant and the proximity of the bodily forces of drives and desires (soon to be discussed) can have a strong and distracting influence.

A diet of other people's images dulls the soul.

It is through our own efforts that external impressions travel into our higher soul regions. We do not do this sitting in front of the television, letting other people's images wash over us. Relaxing in front of the television for short periods of time can bring some balance into our lives, but sitting in front of it continually is a soul-dulling activity. When there is no effort on our part there is no personal growth. Through inner striving we must move impressions up through the regions of our soul while enabling the "I" to connect with the soul's processes.

The higher awareness (third) region of the soul, which it is now possible to develop at this stage of human evolution, is strengthened when we use our will to form conscious intentions and act in the world with purpose. Sometimes it takes great strength of will to act, especially if there are several different ways for us to act. We can take the easy way out and allow our feelings to step up to the base. When we bat with our feelings, pride and ego usually fly.

I went to a podiatrist to have an orthotic made to support my flat feet. He took a plaster cast, made the orthotic and asked me to return with my shoes for a fitting. At this fitting, he described how to fix the orthotic to my shoes by using double-sided tape. He didn't demonstrate this, so I had to use my imagination. It was not easy and the tape kept coming loose, exacerbated by the heat of summer. When I went for my check up he showed me that I had not been using the tape correctly. I suggested to him that it would be much easier if he had supplies of this tape so that he could demonstrate how to use them to his future clients. Then I had to brace myself using all my will forces as he defended his position by saying: "You are the first person in twenty years to mention this." He had placed the responsibility back on me. I thought to myself that perhaps no one had the strength to mention it before.

To avoid expressing ourselves through our lower ego we must continually observe and consider the way we use our will. We need to strengthen our will to be an observer of the situations life presents, rather than diving in and becoming entangled in a sea of emotions and pride. When we do this we only think of ourselves and we cannot place ourselves in the other person's position. If we continually act in the world for self-advantage we will only be dissatisfied. Certainly this is one explanation for the amount of dissatisfaction in the world today.

How can we make the soul more tangible?

Here is a summary of how we touch the world and how the world touches us. We live in the world and perceive it with our senses and our intellect. We form concepts, ideas and images about the world—some we like, some we don't, and this is expressed as feeling. Prompted by our will, and according to our like and dislike, we act by intervening in the processes going on in our environment.

When we sleep all this stops because the soul disconnects with its daily environment and we experience the expressions of our soul in our dreams. Our everyday thinking ceases to function when we dream which is why our dream images are often jumbled.

All these things we are considering are seen to be intangible— dreaming, soul, "I" and spirit—they cannot be seen. However, when we work with the concepts and principles described in this book we can understand them with something that is quite tangible—our reason and logic. By applying healthy human reason and logic, which have been part of us since ancient Greek and Roman times, we can make the intangible tangible. Through reason and logic, by striving to pull our will into our thinking, by grounding our thinking and not floating around in feeling, we can definitely make these intangible things tangible. It can be demonstrated that if thinking has feeling and willing behind it that we will make good decisions. Our thinking will be sound. We won't seek opinions from outside ourselves but will confidently be able to make good choices by ourselves. We will respond to others in a mature and wise way. This means that our I-connection is strong.

Awakening our feeling and our will

When we work to understand and identify the faculties weaving through our soul, feeling and will take on a different quality. Feeling is aroused out of its dreaming, and will is aroused out of its sleeping. We begin to notice that our new experience of will and feeling are quite different. We will have to get used to the new way we use them in our life. They could surprise us! Because this is happening to people as part of human evolution we can observe the transition in some people around us. People are more frequently saying, "Did I do that?" when they achieve something that has not previously been possible for them. The conscious use of will and feeling comes from an inner strength that assists us to move beyond our boundaries. The I-connection brings out our talents and creativity.

It is helpful to see how our language can confuse our understanding of the essential soul functions. For example, "Having a mind to do a thing" is not will—that is thinking and is related to the second soul region where logic and reasoning take place. Someone may say, "That person is wilful." when the person is acting like a child in their feeling levels of like and dislike, not their will. If we are observant we will notice more such statements which misrepresent what is really happening in our soul. To truly understand our soul we need to become clear about such misunderstandings.

It is worth noting that we only have will in these ways:

1. we are born with it; and
2. to the extent our "I" can use our will giving us access to the higher, conscious region of our soul. See chapter 5 for exercises to strengthen the will.

Strengthening our ability to think

Thinking is the most conscious force in our soul and consciousness is the focus of the evolution of humanity. It is not about having a higher consciousness, it is about being conscious. However, much of our every-day thought life is just a duplicate copy of the world outside us. It comes from what we see, hear and experience in our environment, from the people we meet at work and socially, and the things we see in movies or on TV. These things form much of the content of our thoughts and we must become aware that this type of thinking is only a duplicate copy, it is not the original.

We need creative energetic thinking.

Thinking takes energy and we are often too tired or too lazy to invest the energy. Creative and energetic thinking is the greatest tool for strengthening of the I-connection. The more conscious we are, the more observant we will be of everything in our environment. Then when we reflect on our observations and inject them with our own thoughts, our I-connection will give us new understanding. Our "I" will then have greater control over our soul faculties and we will be more harmonious and balanced. When we are placed in a position of thinking a thing through, we should take time to think creatively and originally by putting more energy into the process.

> At the beginning of the year I met with a group of people to decide on the focus of our study group for the year. The leader of the group asked us to do two tasks in a five-minute period. Our response to these two tasks would impact on the whole year. In such a limited time it is only possible to come up with a standard response, a knee-jerk reaction. For me this was very uncreative and I felt that I could only do justice to the task if I could have time to reflect on all the issues.

Thinking is excluded when we act automatically out of habit. Thinking is certainly not about the first thing that comes into our head, for that is usually a replica of past thoughts. The more aware of the habitual processes in our life, the more we can interrupt them and be more creative. In becoming more aware of all the things that we do each day, we will move through our days much more consciously. Obviously we have to do some things automatically or we would never get everything done.

There isn't time to be conscious of everything we do; that is the purpose of habit—so that we can get things done without having to think about all the detail. However, if we can stop and think about some of the things we do habitually and automatically our thinking will be more alive, more energetic.

Thinking can also be exercised by not judging too hastily. If we think about a thing for a while, and sleep on it we will find that we make wise decisions more often.

> If something is upsetting me I seem to forget it about when I go to work because work takes all my attention. But at the end of the working day, when I stop occupying my mind with work, the thing that is upsetting me floods over me again. It is at this point I realise that distracting my thoughts by work has not actually controlled my thinking. Now I am putting effort into developing the ability to control my thinking rather than looking for diversions that distract me from thinking about what is upsetting me.

It is also useful to create a space in our day for new thoughts, a space in which to think about how to act or think or feel about things in new ways. Exploring how to be more creative, even in a busy life, assists our I-connection. Each day brings new opportunities to strive for inner strength, and by thinking about our I-connection, we can discover ways to recognise how it works in our individual lives.

Developing a working relationship with our soul and "I"

Our "I" is our inner strength.

There are many ways to identify the I-connection. For instance, we may feel our "I" standing in our being like the mast of a tall ship. We can also experience it as calm and peace as we try to raise our emotions to a higher level. For example, if we feel animosity for someone, we can try to lighten that feeling and make it less intense. If we can't eliminate it but can move to a milder dislike, or to a feeling of mild annoyance, then our "I" is connecting and assisting us to be more objective. Another approach is to find one thing to like about the person. It is when we do things like this that we can become more aware of the experience of our "I" in our soul. This will add strength to thinking. It will also assist us to create new habits, think about things in new ways, and then our "I" will be in charge of our soul more often. This will also prevent the soul from excluding the "I" which it is often inclined to do.

When we begin to feel the benefits of exercising control in our soul other interesting observations can be made. We will discover that we can't actually think about thinking; we can only view our thinking. While we are absorbed in a thought our "I" is not present. In other words, after the thought has been thought, our "I" can look at what we thought. If we can have a working understanding of this we will be quite sure what is the work of our soul and what is the work of our "I", which also assists us to recognise how they can work harmoniously together. We can't have a living understanding of our soul and "I" as they operate in the world unless we develop a working relationship with them. Our task is to become a conscious participator in our soul life, not a spectator or slave of it. The soul can be a surging force sweeping us from one thing to the next unless we allow our "I" to intervene.

One of the main reasons we can be unsettled in this world is because without our understanding and participation, our soul and our "I" carry us automatically through life. Usually, if we do feel them at work within us it is only dimly, like a shadowy phantom. This is what many people experience at this stage of human evolution.

Our experience of the world happens in this way:

1. We perceive the world through our senses;
2. We experience the world through our soul;
3. We understand the world through our spirit, our "I".

The interaction of the soul's processes can be summarised as follows:

◊ Outer objects compel us and stimulate our thinking;
◊ Our thinking determines our feeling and willing/effort;
◊ Thinking stamps onto feeling where pleasure is based;
◊ Through feeling our will is aroused.

It may seem ridiculous to list these things that we do everyday in our life. However by understanding what is at work we understand ourselves more fully.

The rhythmic process in the soul regions and soul faculties

We relate to the world through a rhythmic process. We take things in from the world, we withdraw to make sense of what we have taken in, and then we express something out into the world again as a result. We can represent it in this way -

1	IMPULSE/DESIRE/INSTINCT	)	HAVING
2	LOGIC/REACTION/MIND	O	BEING
3	AWARENESS/WISDOM/COMPREHENSION	(	DOING

What happens is this; in the first region of the soul we open ourselves to the world, we reach out and we receive. It is a like a soul-hand reaching out, a soul gesture, to the outside world. Our soul reaches out and takes impulses into it - colours, sounds, smells, shapes etc.

Then our soul closes up within itself and mulls over these things, it reflects, ponders and reasons. In our soul we internalise the experiences we took in from the outside world. We compare the new impulses with the ideas we already have about things. We compare them with past impulses, experiences and images. So if we see a cat, in the first soul region we say, "I've got another picture like that, it's furry, it purrs, it's soft and it scratches." It is this sequence of ideas that is the recognition that builds up our knowledge.

In this way we come to realise how everything in our soul is in continual movement, that a continual process takes place. The desires that rise up from our body are constantly absorbed into our feelings and judgments continually give rise to mental images.

What our "I" sees, for example, a cat, we *feel* from past experience, we *judge* from the present and then we *form an image*, and keep forming it until it fits the thing that we saw, in this case, a cat. Through our "I" we then face that enduring image of the cat.

When we have an awareness, what we call a deeper understanding, it means that the information we have gathered and compared in the first two regions of our soul can be used by us to act in the world, to express ourselves outwards again. With that new knowledge, our soul reaches out into the world and changes it. Everything we do changes and creates the world.

Pruning a tree is a good example as previously mentioned: If we prune a tree we change the world forever. The scenery doesn't look the same. We see the overhanging branch, we think about it and we decide to prune it and the shape of the tree is changed by our action, unlikely to ever look the same again.

It is important for the soul to breathe.

These three: see, think, prune are channels for the "I" and the soul to express themselves in the world. Then our feeling, thinking and willing/action can be experienced by others. We can see that these faculties in the soul have a rhythmic/breathing action, an inhalation/breathing in, a holding of our breath for a moment, and then an exhalation/breathing out. See diagram 1.3.

We have all experienced being in a situation where we stop and hold our breath. Something happens that makes us stand still for a moment. This standing still occurs in the second soul region. It is as if we spin around on the spot. We try to think what to do but we can't act. As we know, if we hold our breath for too long we will die; it is just as unhealthy for our soul to stop like this for too long.

Instead, we have to become aware of the rhythmic, breathing action of having, being and doing; not staying in one or the other area for too long. By raising our experiences to the third soul region we can act; and by engaging our "I" we can act wisely.

To summarise; our soul's response to life often happens automatically. When we are more conscious of our "I" we can influence the way our soul responds. The activity of our soul is expressed through our body, and can be guided by our "I". The more mature our I-connection is, the wiser our expressions will be.

It should be noted that it is possible to discipline our soul and body to act in certain ways; this does not point to a mature I-connection but to an automatic or learned response in our body and soul. When the "I" is mature and we are conscious of its presence, we can make wise decisions in many different circumstances and do this on the run.

The interaction between the body, soul and spirit

Now we can look more closely at how the body, soul and spirit interact. Diagram 3.3 below shows the inner/outer perspective of the soul. Remember that the perspective we have been considering till now is lower to higher: feeling, thinking willing. This perspective of inner to outer means that willing is deep inside, feeling is in the middle predominating and thinking is at the interface to the outside world. Through thinking we are united with the world. Feeling connects us with our inner-self and we become aware that we are individuals. Will connects us with our body.

In the diagram, the soul is represented by the circle, the *drives* of the physical organs are pictured outside the soul's processes, although we

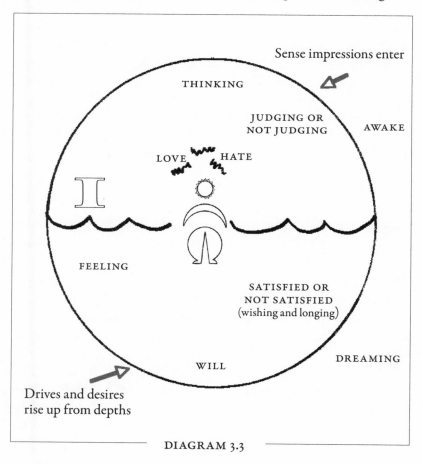

DIAGRAM 3.3

must continually remember that the soul is all around us, in and through us. The body speaks to the soul by communicating its needs. When the organs in our body speak to the soul they create *drives* in us. Our d*rives* are things like hunger, thirst and the regulation of warmth. Our *drives* are necessary to keep our body alive, to sustain our physical existence.

Triggered by these *drives*, *desires* arise up out of the depths of our physical body. The purpose of desires is to engage the soul and keep it active. When the *drives* become *desires* the desires then alert us so that we know that we are hungry and that we should eat, or that we are cold and need warmth.

If the *drives* connect up with the *desires* but then do not reach our soul regions, we wouldn't be able to act, to use our will. So we would feel hungry but we would not eat, we would feel the cold but we wouldn't warm ourselves. Note that the will in the diagram is just over the threshold of the soul where the body and soul meet. *Desires* are therefore first experienced as urges at the interface of our body and soul. This becomes slightly confusing because we have been associating the first region of the soul, the impulse region, with feeling yet here we are speaking of the will to do a thing. With careful thought these two different perspectives will make sense.

We can become familiar with the force of the will through hunger.

Our most basic desires or urges are hunger and thirst. The best time to experience the force of our will is when we are hungry. We know that we have to control these impulses of hunger so that we deal with our hunger in a human way, not an animal way. We do this by infusing our *will* with *thinking*. If we do not infuse our will with thinking, we could just eat anything or snatch someone else's food from them as animals can do.

When the *will* is fully permeated by *thinking* then we can add *feeling* to it. At this point, we may ask ourselves: What would we like to eat? How will we eat? We may think of people living in impoverished conditions who do not have enough to eat, or we may think of all the effort from those people who made it possible for us to eat the food. (This is another example of the difference between humans and animals.) We might wonder about the effect of genetically modified food or food produced by people motivated by greed. What effect would this have on us? Perhaps it could affect our *will*, weaken it and make us less conscious? Or is there a difference between food grown in another country, rather than in our own garden? These are the thoughts of an awakened soul.

It is not so hard to become conscious of the *drives* and *desires* that rise up within our body. Then we begin to notice how often we act on an urge without thinking. This can happen when the tools of the "I": feeling, thinking and willing are not being used by the "I" but take their own course according to the likes and dislikes of the soul in its dreamy state.

Thinking, feeling and will are about timing.

We make irrational decisions whenever we let the wrong soul faculty take centre stage at the wrong time. These faculties have a certain sequence for each situation, but unless we are conscious of our *drives* and *desires*, our faculties can be used in the wrong order. For example, what happens if our feeling comes in too soon? The *drives* and subsequently the *desires* (lower urges) rise and instead of infusing the *will* with *thinking*, they infuse the will with our likes and dislikes, our *feeling*. When this happens we remain in the lower soul regions and like children, and some dementia patients, we can make irrational decisions about what to eat—such as eating lollies instead of dinner. By observing children we can easily see the elements of the unawakened soul at work. Part of growing up is to learn how to control our soul regions, but during this process we can easily use them out of order. This is why we can say that our parents and carers stand-in for the "I" during this time. Obviously the quality of this 'standing-in' will have a great effect on our adult life.

The life cycle of the soul

We can trace the life cycle of a *drive* which is created in the depths of our body and see that it becomes a *desire* once it reaches our soul regions. *Desire* then becomes *will*, the motivator, in the regions of our soul closest to our body. We can't be conscious of the activity of this will because it is unconscious, asleep and it should stay that way because who wants to be conscious of our bodily processes like digestion? The *drive* moves through these stages: from *drive* to *desire*, to *will*, to *feelings*. When it reaches our feelings we become dreamily aware of it according to how awake our soul is.

We spend most of our life in the middle region of the soul; bubbling along in a dreamy state, bobbing around in the ocean of feelings. This is why the middle region appears in the diagram like a wavy sea. Feelings alone are all about like or dislike, love or hate/fear. Towards the end of the cycle the *desire* moves up to the region where decision-making or judging occur. Here we are awake and thinking enters the process.

Another way to look at this process is to think of the gears in a motor vehicle. When we are in first gear we are moving with the basic *desire*. As we said, desires arise from unknown depths outside the awareness of our soul. Take the example of needing to be kissed by someone we love. This desire can bubble up in our body towards our soul where we will feel and think about it and apply our will to it.

Wishing and longing are unsatisfied desires.

As the *desire* enters our soul and becomes *will* we are motivated to find the person who can give us the kiss. This desire for a kiss then exists in potential to be satisfied, otherwise it remains unsatisfied. We may realise that it is not possible for it to be satisfied at the moment. Perhaps the person who could kiss us is unavailable, they may be in another city or country, or perhaps we haven't even met them yet. The desire can then become a wish or a longing, in which case it is a liberated desire and it is placed in the future to be fulfilled later on. If the desire is neither satisfied nor unsatisfied, it remains in a waiting bay to be satisfied as a *wish* or a longing. Wishes and longings can work against us if they are too strong because they interrupt the soul's life cycle. If we focus on what cannot be satisfied we become very dissatisfied.

Continuing with the image of changing the gears of a car, if the desire remains immediate, seeking satisfaction, then it goes into second gear and enters the realm of *feeling*. This is the middle area of the soul, the dreamy middle ground where we spend most of our time. Quite often the *feeling* is that we can't be bothered. Here, we might say to ourselves: 'Yes I want a kiss but I can't be bothered putting any effort into it' or 'Yes, I am hungry but I can't be bothered to get up and go to the kitchen' or 'Yes I am hungry but I can't be bothered to cook, I'll phone for a pizza.' This is where we can leave ourselves open to the prevailing influences of the automatic life of the soul. That is our enemy.

Feelings are modified desires.

Our desires can be given more fuel by *feelings* as we imagine how good the kiss could be, or we may even realise that we don't need the kiss after all. In other words we modify the desire. Remember not to confuse this middle of the soul where feeling reigns with the second region of the soul we spoke about earlier which is the logic/reasoning region.

If we decide to continue our journey and change into third gear, we enter the area of the soul where love and hate are found. This is a focal area of the soul where misunderstanding arises about the inner nature of the human being. Love and hate polarise us and tear us in two. The healthy soul is able to engage in the tensions of inner life and resist the temptation to flee from them. It is only when we experience both extremes of the polarity that arise in our soul that we are propelled along in life. The emphasis is on 'experience', we shouldn't dwell on either of the extremes of a polarity.

If we lean over to one side (all love), or the other (all hate), we will go nowhere and become slaves to the automatic soul forces. We have to experience the tearing of the two, this polarisation of the two before we can be propelled upwards properly—just like kites need a certain amount of resistance to fly. If we don't meet the resistance by using our will-filled thinking, we just flop into loving or hating, liking or disliking, being brave or being fearful, oscillating from one to the other.

Taking responsibility for self.

In third gear we can propel ourselves along the highway or off a cliff—the choice is ours. We can take responsibility for, and conscious control of, our soul or we can resort to dependency therapies or medication that can interrupt the connection between our body, soul and spirit.

The importance of the process of judging

At this point in our journey we start to seriously weigh things up and ask ourselves: 'How much do I want this kiss and how will I get it?' If we successfully navigate this road in third gear we can move into fourth gear. Now we are in the area of the soul where we make decisions based on our ability to judge. In this region we make right or wrong decisions.

However, judging is an active process experienced in the soul, not an end result. Through judging we re-live our life at the same time that we are living it. In other words, at the same time we are experiencing present experiences, we are re-experiencing past experiences. The basis of judging happens in this past-present process. It is helpful to use the word 'judging' rather than judgment whenever possible as a reminder that it is a continual process.

In the process of judging we first reach a *conclusion* (will I or won't I have the kiss). Something enters into our soul from outside and we reach a conclusion, then we make a *judgment* (who from); from these two processes we form a *concept* (kissing is best when it is with the one we love). Of course, we are not always aware that we continuously carrying out this activity; but it is only by means of this activity that we can live our life consciously instead of automatically. The more we are able to develop new concepts the less we use old ones. Also, this is the process which enables us to communicate with each other through speech. Therefore the quality of our verbal communication is directly related to the agility of our soul and the strength of our I-connection.

When considering the mechanism of judging in the soul, it is interesting to consider that the Greek word which Aristotle would have used for 'judgment' is krisis. 'Krisis' speaks of a separating process; a decision-making process of pulling an issue apart and putting it back together again. In short, by pulling things apart and putting them back together again we reach a conclusion, make a judgment and form a concept. This is about weighing things, which is why judgment is often represented by scales.

Judging experiences all sides equally.

Judging is not about taking one position or another; judging is about a continual weighing up, visiting both sides, not staying on one side. When both sides of the scale are balanced, then judging can occur. It is interesting to discover that everything we face in life can equally be proved as right as it can be contradicted as wrong. We must let the pros AND the cons merge in our soul with equal weight, not one outweighing the other. Compare it to breathing in and breathing out—both must be equal; there would be nasty consequences if we breathed in more than we breathed out.

If we can manage to achieve this judging movement more often in our soul then we become more certain. We will be able to discern what is good and what is bad more quickly. We become a better judge. It must be emphasised that judging is something we do, not something we rest on. It is an active thing that is continually modified by new information. It always involves some reflecting or pondering. Judging assists us to test the authenticity of anything new that enters into our soul. There are, however, some watch-points. We should try to avoid remaining in our old position and judging from there. In other words, we must actively move forward into the new and judge from that new position. This requires a certain amount of strength and courage. Many judgments are made by sitting back in a comfortable old recliner position instead of jumping to our feet and stepping into the new experience.

Delayed decisions are wise decisions.

In our journey we have come to this area of the soul where we make decisions . . . or not make them. To make the right decisions we need to be wide-awake. (Notice where the words 'asleep', 'dreaming' and 'awake' are positioned on the right side of the diagram.) We are not aware of our *drives* and *desires* as they approach our will because they are asleep in the depths of our being, outside the awareness of our soul. At the other end of the cycle we decide: 'Will I take a kiss from anyone and have it now, or wait for the person who can give me the best kiss?' When the desire reaches the judgement area we may think, "I just have to have the kiss, I don't care *who* gives it to me." This part of the cycle is where poor decision-making can occur.

Try not to make an important
decision on the same day as the issue arises.

Remember that when the desire for a kiss first arose we were not conscious of it, we were asleep to it. When the desire entered our feeling regions we started to become conscious of it, but as if we were dreaming. Then when the desire rises up to where a decision can be made we are very aware of the desire; we are wide awake to it. Now we ask ourselves, "Will I decide or not, and what will I decide?" The soul actually likes to be in this continual flux because it dislikes making decisions. It is the human spirit that likes continuity and it is the influence of the "I" that assists us to reach good decisions.

In the diagram, note that the "I" stands above the perpetual motion of the ocean of the soul. This is why, when forced to make a decision, we should sleep on it overnight.

The quality of the judging will be according to the level of involvement of the "I".

Also notice in the diagram that thinking is placed to the left and slightly higher than judging. Our thinking assists the judging process—rightly or wrongly. The quality of the judging will be according to the level of in-volvement of the "I". If the "I" enters into the process then we are in over-drive and we speed up the highway in freedom.

Thoughts that pester us, such as: "Why didn't I do this?" or "Why didn't I say that?" are simply old willing; the old desire that went through all the processes above and reached a different decision, or we didn't decide at all. The only way to get rid of this dissatisfaction is to replace it with something new that can be decided differently.

Thinking is mature willing and willing is youthful thinking.

A desire that has arisen in us, and has been thought through to its fulfil-ment is a mature thought. Conversely, a desire that is not thought through is immature. An immature desire operates within the region of the soul that is asleep and can lead to unwise action; then we can act without thinking. This explains why teenagers, who haven't got full possession of the regions of the soul, often do impulsive and unwise things.

Guidelines for judging

Judging is an area of great personal difficulty and societal misunder-standing. How can we decide what is true and what is false, what is good and what it bad? Many of us would still agree today with the philosopher Henry Thoreau, who said in the 19th century: *"The greater part of what my neighbours call good I believe in my soul to be bad . . .".* Judgment is inflicted on us from every side of life and we are justified to ask about the quality of this judgment. The freedom and ability to decide for ourselves is not always recognised or given. Who decides what is right and what is wrong? Who should decide? Do those who take authority (government, church, parents . . .) themselves do what they enforce, preach or say?

Here are some guidelines for judging that lead to good decision making:

1. postpone judgement;
2. visualise the consequences of any possible action;
3. visualise the consequence of no action;
4. stop thinking about the matter;
5. sleep on it, if possible for three nights;
6. on the third morning repeat the two visualisations;
7. then, make a decision and accept full responsibility for it.

Although we may strive to make the right decisions, we do not always achieve this. Nonetheless, without disharmony and error we would not progress. The reason the soul learns through mistakes (and also through illness) is because these things take the soul beyond the normal limits of daily life. So harmony is disrupted by disharmony and then harmony is restored—it is an upward spiral.

We are strengthened by our mistakes.

It is important that when we are faced with the need to judge, we remember not to judge too hastily. Our I-connection depends on it; whenever we judge hastily our "I" is excluded. Our consideration needs to be free of the automatic, unconscious processes in our life. This is assisted by the recommended daily exercise of creating a space within us for new thoughts, new ideas and new actions. Above all we need to strive for inner strength, to be peaceful and to refine our feelings and emotions. All these will lead to balanced judging.

The importance of experiencing powerlessness.

There is a final matter for consideration in this journey of self-understanding. As we start to experience the inner workings of our soul a feeling of powerlessness can arise within us. As we become aware of how often our soul's automatic processes take over we can feel powerless to do anything about this. There is, however, a secret in this feeling of powerlessness. If we allow ourselves to experience it our I-connection is strengthened. Essentially the feeling of power in our soul is usually connected with our egotistical feelings. If we can quieten them down by accepting the feeling of powerlessness, we will suddenly become aware of the presence of our "I" in our soul and how it has a different sense of 'power'. This is the quiet confidence and self esteem that was discussed in chapter 2.

If we apply all this information in our daily lives, if we make a habit of vigorously thinking things through as we move through life, we will be strong and vital citizens. Each of us is different and these processes work in each of us differently. Only we can understand the working of it for our self. This means that how one person applies the information in this book is not good for all. The framework of the information is solid and lends itself to being adapted and personalised easily.

With this detailed view of the soul in terms of feeling, thinking and will it will be useful to look in more detail at the three soul regions as they form the evolving consciousness of the human being.

Chapter 4: Three Soul Regions: impulse, reasoning, awareness

If we are to understand ourselves, to truly become mates with our soul, we need a more detailed picture of the inner activity of our soul life. As we consider our soul it is important to remember that our "I", our self, experiences life through our soul, which is in turn expressed through our body. The picture of the "I" as the artist, the soul his work of art and the body as the canvas is a good way to remember how these parts of our being work together.

Different cultures have different soul moods.

Our soul is coloured by all the different influences in our lives; our environment, our family, our friends, our work, events and experiences, our country and culture, and even by the climate. This author is Australian and views life from an Australian perspective. The Asian, Spanish or American person will view things differently. Hopefully the following detail about the different soul regions will assist people from all cultures and countries to understand how they express themselves through the different tones of their soul.

There can be no question of racism in the study of our soul, but simply the recognition of different soul influences and different soul moods. In fact, when we pursue this knowledge we can also discover that some people feel more comfortable with those of the same soul mood, others relate easily to a variety of soul moods. The stronger our I-connection the more easily we relate "I" to "I", less influenced by soul moods.

We have explored how the three soul regions relate specifically to the three soul faculties; feeling, thinking and intent. The way we feel is related to the way we receive *impulses*, the way we think is found in our ability to *reason* and our intentions reveal the level of our *awareness*. These are characteristic regions of our soul which, in this book, we call *impulse*, *reasoning* and *awareness* regions.

Some people work out of a balance of all three regions; others express themselves predominately from one area. We can certainly move from one to the other at lightening speed moment by moment throughout the day depending on the prevailing circumstances. Our observations will confirm that some people are *feeling* people, others are *thinkers* and some others are more *aware*, more conscious, more knowing. The optimum is to work in a balanced way in the upper regions of our soul so that our intentions are guided and supported by the clear thoughts and warm feelings.

In our brief look at these regions in chapter 1, we saw how they develop as we mature. In the young person feeling dominates. As we mature thinking is added to feeling. Hopefully by the time we reach our fifties all three regions work harmoniously and with agility, and wisdom prevails.

Until we are conscious of the way our soul
works much of what our soul does is automatic.

While we examine these three different regions of our soul, it is important to realise that even though we may express ourselves predominately through one region, the three soul regions continually interact and interweave. Until we become more aware of the activity of these regions, the interaction is unconscious. When our awareness increases we can influence these soul processes.

The first step to experiencing our soul is to place ourselves inside the weaving activity. This is easier to do with stronger feelings like anger. We can participate in anger as it rises up within us and we can become conscious of how it is apprehended by thinking. If a friend offends us there is always a moment when we choose to be outraged or to be forgiving. The more quickly we are able to think, and the more objective we can be and the more rational our response. If our rational thoughts don't intervene the feeling can take on a life of its own and we can have a tantrum which may ruin a good friendship. If, through our thoughts, we experience the love we have for our friend, the anger can be quickly converted to love and forgiveness.

Building an image of our soul activity.

We can also become more aware of how feeling, when added to dry and abstract thinking, influences the way we act. We can also see how feeling assists us with the decision to act or not. These feelings, while influencing our will, can be further modified by thinking. If we think we should weed the garden, it isn't until we feel the enjoyment that would come from the result of weeding the garden, that we are actually motivated to do the work. The anticipation of the satisfaction is then interrupted when we start to think about how we will do the task.

Unless we can identify how the regions and faculties of the soul work in our daily life, our understanding of these things will remain theoretical and less meaningful. It is very helpful to build active imaginations or images of the way the different soul activities work together; the more vivid the pictures the better.

One picture that can be helpful is to visualise a pressure gauge which moves up and down as the different soul regions are accessed. We can choose colours for these soul activities, for example, red for feelings/*impulse* region, yellow for thoughts/*reasoning* region, and blue for intentions/*awareness* region. Then imagine how much yellow is in the red when we moderate a feeling with a thought. Then, how much blue flows through when we draw on our will levels. Better still is when we become more conscious of these processes naturally throughout the day.

We can build a more complete picture of our soul's processes by understanding in more detail what happens in each soul region and how each region interacts with the others. This, of course, is influenced by the strength of our I-connection. When we look at each region, always remember that our soul has two essential modes of operation:

◊ one is semi-conscious and automatic;
◊ the other is conscious and I-connected.

These conditions can fluctuate from one extreme to the other. To understand it best we must try to compare this information with our own experiences of our soul and "I". The following analysis uses the higher/lower view of the three regions of the soul (feeling, thinking, willing in that order) instead of the inner/outer (willing, feeling, thinking) perspective used in the life cycle of the soul in the previous chapter.

I. THE IMPULSE SOUL

What happens in the impulse region

Feelings arise in the impulse region of our soul.

The impulse soul region is the home of sense impressions, sensations, impulses, and also this is where instincts, desires, and emotions are given dignity.

In this region we find the holding bay for all the impulses that we take in from the outside world through our *senses*—our eyes, ears, nose, fingers, skin, tongue etc. This is the area of our soul where living *sensations* enter. It is here that we register things like pleasure or pain and bodily comfort or discomfort. Here we can enjoy the touch of a loved one, the warmth of a smile, or flinch at the prick of a thorn or the pain of stubbing our toe. This is where our feelings are dominant.

It is this region of our soul that is active in the first flush of falling in love when we want the sound of our lover's voice to wash over us as we take in all the sensations from them. After a time, when we start to think things over in the second, reasoning soul region, we can have a different view of the person we have been consumed with.

As emphasised before, to create balance in our life, our constant goal is to use all the regions of our soul as a team and not act predominately out of one region.

The impulse soul is not the natural habitat of the "I".

If we remember that the "I" is closely associated with thinking we realise that the "I" works quite dimly in the first region of our soul. It is here that egotistical passions can emerge if we don't push sensations up to the next region of our soul where we can think about them. In this lowest soul region we experience how feeling on its own, without thinking, can make us self-centred—this is primarily because of the weak influence from the "I". Then we don't want others to have what we have, like a cat that has caught a mouse and hisses if we approach, or similarly, a dog with a bone will growl. Our sense of justice can be weak unless thinking comes into the process. We live in these regions when we do not put effort into life. By effort is meant using our will to infuse the sensations or impulses with thinking and will so that we think things through thoroughly.

In these lower regions of our soul where impulses arise, we are hardly aware of ourselves. We lose ourselves in the impulses and sensations; there is diminished control, no thinking, little awareness, as if no one is in charge. Our actions are automatic. We can strengthen the "I" forces in this region by being more conscious of how we feel, by being less forgetful and by trying to infuse our feelings with thoughts.

Our soul can be lazy.

This type of forgetfulness or lack of awareness results from soul-laziness. By exerting ourselves to think, we immediately engage the second region of our soul. If we have not made a habit of this throughout our life then in old age we will be more forgetful and operate in an automatic way. The roots of dementia may be found here. If we exercise our will forces—intentions based on awareness—when we are younger, always pushing ourselves to become more conscious, we will have a vibrant soul in old age and our soul faculties will be alive and vital. We cannot work on our will when we are older, just as it would be difficult to suddenly take up tennis when we are 80 if we hadn't played it when we were younger.

This is the region of living sensations.

The impulse region is the region of pure experience; this is where living sensations are produced. The first feelings that come from a touch, a sound or a taste are vivid in this region. Once these impulses enter into us we reproduce the impressions, creating a personal image of them. The richness of experiences depends on the involvement of our whole being; the other soul regions and the "I". When we raise the impulse into our second soul region where we think about it, the sensation will remain vivid if we use our will to keep the feelings alive. If the feelings fade while we are thinking about the impression, then the impression becomes cold and dry.

The soul mood of the Spanish or Latin cultures reveals the nature of this soul region: passionate, laid back, colourful, artistic and in touch with their senses. As mentioned in chapter 1, we can trace the development of the human soul through the various cultures throughout history.

The nature of our impulse soul reveals our attitude to life. The way our inner nature participates in life is directly related to the development of this region of our soul. Whether we are harmoniously adjusted to life or not has its roots here. If we are hesitant to engage with the impressions that enter us it means that we may not let life touch us fully.

Processing the outside world

Whatever enters our senses is first processed in the impulse soul region.

We know that through our senses impressions from the outside world enter into us. These senses for the most part are directly connected to our body, our eyes, ears, nose etc., rather than our soul. (This is dealt with in more detail in the Appendix.) We become conscious of the impressions that enter us because our soul makes 'sense' of the image it receives in the second soul region.

Compare the senses of the body to a baker gathering the ingredients to make bread. The baker gathers everything together to prepare the loaf. In this way the baker represents our senses. The loaf represents the mental image created in the second soul region. When the image is as fully formed as possible it is then absorbed by the "I". We can say that the "I" takes possession of the image. The "I" takes the image of the bread from the baker (body) in the soul where it can be used, where something can be made of it. We could say that;

1. In the first soul region we feel something about the bread, for example, we like it or we don't like it.
2. In the second soul region we think about the bread, for example, about its goodness or freshness.
3. In the third soul region we become aware of its value, for example, whether to eat it and how much to eat.

It is very helpful to continually build these types of images so that our experience more fully the nature of our being.

If the impressions entering our soul are not
grasped by thinking they fade and die like a rainbow.

We don't always apply our feelings, thoughts and intentions to the images we receive. When the "I" takes possession of an image, this occurs in the first soul region. Here the natural course of events is for the images to fade and die like a rainbow. Think of a rainbow in the sky, it is there one minute and it's gone the next. The same happens in the impulse region of our soul. Before the image fades we have the opportunity to grasp it. Thinking is the grasping which happens in the reasoning region of our soul (the second region). Here we recreate the impression, make a copy of it, otherwise it fades and dies, it is gone and therefore forgotten.

This is exactly what happens when we meet a new person. When we are introduced to them we often quickly forget their name because our senses are so busy taking in all the impressions from the newly met person; how they look, what they are wearing, the sound of their voice, how we feel about them etc. The first region of our soul is so busy with all these new impressions it can't manage to engage the second region of our soul so that we can register the words of their name and recall it later. Many of the tricks to remembering people's names are nothing more than a trigger to engage the second soul region through thinking.

This also explains why we forget some of the impulses that come to us. When we receive an image, if we can't make anything of it, it fades away. Or if we aren't paying attention or we are disinterested; the images don't reach the middle regions of our soul and they fade and die. This is explains why two people can witness an event and give two different accounts of it. All through our life each image that enters into us is either kept or discarded. Some are more meaningful than others. We must build a rich imagery in our soul that can connect to new images otherwise new impressions are lost to us. In this context it is interesting to think about the Australian aboriginal woman who thought that the first truck she saw was a moving rock.

Medication can interfere with our soul's functioning.

It is also in this area that old people or people on medication can lose images. Their soul is not pliable enough to take hold of the image. Medication can prevent their soul from grasping the image because it interferes with the I-connection. What in fact happens is that the image tries to enter the soul but if the soul cannot take hold of it, then the image sinks back down into their body where it came from.

The elderly often just let external impressions, one after the other, wash over them. It is easy to see how these impressions can quickly fade and die if we do not engage our thinking processes from the second region of our soul. We often hear old people say that if we keep our mind active we will not get Dementia. This is the proof of that.

A geriatric nurse tells of an incident where an old lady immediately forgot the birthday cake she had just shared with her friends and angrily accused them of not giving her one. There was no proof because they had all eaten the cake. The nurse had to ask them all to say that there had been a birthday cake and that they had all eaten a piece.

Those of us who energetically involve all the regions of our soul in our daily life should reach old age with the agility of soul to process most of the external impressions that enter into us.

Within each region of our soul is a higher and lower expression.

In the first region of our soul where our feelings originate we will see that these feelings can be expressed in an *instinctive* animalistic way or in a *refined* human way. We will notice that we move between these two poles. We can be a raging bull or we can take the fire of the anger and use it to achieve a higher outcome. In the lower regions of the impulse soul we can automatically react if someone upsets us; in the higher regions we can be more rational and respond in a measured and thoughtful way.

An example of the difference is the parent who screams at their child for being clumsy and breaking a glass or the parent who is understanding and says, "Never mind, accidents happen". The thinking parent may encourage the child to use an unbreakable cup.

While we say that feelings belong in the first soul region, they are also expressed in the second soul regions, but in a different way. Feelings are more superficial in the impulse soul; they become more inward in the second soul region when reasoning is applied.

In this first region of our soul we also find our sense of beauty. The most heightened sense of beauty happens when our I-connection is strongest. When we re-create or re-live our sense impressions we can also give them meaning. It is in this region that we first experience our inner mind. In terms of our evolving consciousness, it was in pre-Christian times that we first began to experience our impulse soul and for the first time we had an inner experience of ourselves. This is the time when

Aristotle began to map out the different regions of the soul mentioned in chapter 1. He was, in fact, charting a new human experience.

What the "I" experiences in the impulse soul

The impulse soul is where the "self", the "I" experiences all the feelings that rise up within our being: the surging sea of instincts, passions and *desires* in their extremes, for example, like or dislike, pleasure or pain, as well as the *higher feelings* of love and peace. The more mature the I-connection the higher the expression of this first soul region. Because the "I" strives towards objectivity it is not at home in this region of our soul. (The native territory of the "I" is the next region of our soul, the region of reasoning.) As we connect with life our experiences can be very subjective in this region.

We need to experience anger but shouldn't necessarily express it.

In the impulse soul the "I" can use the inner experience of anger to develop love. It is important for us to experience anger within our being; it often indicates that our I-connection is strengthening. Not that our anger increases, but that we become conscious of it. If we have developed strength in this area of our soul we can transform the anger into a higher expression; if there is weakness then we will express the anger. Transmuted anger is love in action.

> In a counselling session I could see changes occurring in my client. His I-connection was developing and he spoke of becoming more conscious of his anger. He was starting to see himself more clearly and there was a noticeable change in him. In the session he realised how angry he felt towards a friend and had thoughts of punishing him. When we explored this further it was revealed that the friend was reflecting to my client how my client used to be, which he is now trying to move away from.
>
> I could see how the "I" increases the tension in people and gives them the opportunity to turn anger into love. My client then said when he saw his motives to retaliate, "I am not really being loving there am I?" I could see how important objectivity can be; to look at situations as if they are happening to someone else can be helpful. At the same time, trying to experience the other person as yourself.

At the other extreme we often read in the press that anger is increasingly turning into rage on the road. This news report is an alarming example.

> The driver of a Holden Commodore with faulty brake lights was turning into his driveway when he stopped to give way to a cyclist. The driver of the Toyota behind him became enraged. He pulled into the driveway behind the Commodore to vent his anger and at the same time a toddler got out of the first car and was wedged between the two cars. The boy suffered massive internal injuries and died several hours later in hospital. The driver of the Toyota was taken to hospital with a broken arm and bruises after being dragged from his car and attacked with a cricket bat and rake by members of the toddler's family. Stunned relatives yesterday struggled to understand how a trivial traffic dispute could lead to the death of a little boy.

The impulses in the first region of our soul can be highly active; moderation is the key regulator. In the measured response to the outside world, the impulse soul becomes strong and increasingly connected to the "I".

When making decisions the more conscious our response the better, then we will not act instinctively by using old patterns of behaviour. The "I" can be completely disconnected from this area of our soul if we do not think things through before we act.

Difficulties encountered in the impulse soul

Within this region is the possibility to act in response to outer demands rather than our own inner convictions (which arise when the whole soul works as a team with the "I"). When under pressure, we are likely to operate from this region of our soul, because we don't have time to think, we just react out of habit. Swamped in feelings, we cannot think things through or put things in perspective.

We can be too blasé in the impulse soul region.

We are inclined to feel secure in this region. However, by acting predominately out of this soul region we can do the most damage to ourselves and others. This is because we can be surrounded by, and swept along by, a feeling. Once thinking and wisdom combine with feeling, we are not so unquestioning.

When our I-connection is weak, and when the other two higher soul regions are not active by remaining in the background; we can be slavishly subject to this region of our soul. We can recognise this most easily in our automatic responses. Are we positive or negative? Do we habitually say, "That will never work" or, do we often say, "That's a possibility"?

The instinctive behaviour patterns of the impulse soul region can be seen in the salesperson who only thinks of the immediate benefit to himself from sale that can be made today, without thinking of the ongoing orders that could result by considering the customer's needs ahead of his own commission. The salesman who is swayed by self-interest often does not get repeat orders.

A weakness in this region of our soul means the lack of energy to try new solutions. To do something in a new way requires strength of soul and an "I" that is fully engaged in the process. Because the "I" is not at home in the lowest region of our soul more effort is required. If we mostly operate from this region of our soul we will have an underdeveloped or lazy intelligence. We are not exercising our mind, our thinking ability, because we don't engage the second soul region. In this sense, intelligence is not so much an inherited disposition but an acquired ability.

Pain and anxiety have a purpose.

If we persist in living in the lower levels of our soul where the body's influences are strongest we will be more inclined to experience pain and suffering. This is the natural habitat of pain and suffering. By exercising our soul muscles we will see, not an absence of pain, suffering and anxiety but a different view of it. Insight can shine like the sun into our pain and illumine our understanding. Then the purpose of pain can be realised and we become more conscious of the purpose of life's lessons. This in turn builds a strong I-connection.

The lowest region of our soul is the one that we have worked with longest. Being the lowest soul region, the responses that come from here are deep seated and hard to change. Although it takes effort to control and guide this area, we cannot ignore or negate our feelings either. Thinking without feelings is cold and abstract.

Historically speaking, if mankind had not developed beyond this region of soul, we would not have an advanced scientific understanding or the modern technology that has developed from using the second, reasoning soul region.

Harmonious function of the impulse soul

If the first soul region is functioning in a balanced way it fosters a positive, warm, extravert and active attitude. For optimum performance the balance must exist not only within the impulse region but extend to the two higher soul regions in tandem with the "I".

When the impulse soul is functioning harmoniously, we have an even emotional tone and our feelings are moderate in normal circumstances. We are open to new experiences and can handle a variety of situations with a certain degree of confidence (regardless of the effort that may take). If this is the case, we can say that the impulse area of our soul is healthy, mature and not childlike which it can be if it is underdeveloped.

If we feel an inner emptiness, a lack of enthusiasm, if we feel out of touch with other people in the world there are some simple things we can do to restore the balance. We can do some observation exercises; we can look out of the window or go for a walk and then write down all the things we saw. Painting, drawing and clay modelling, singing, movement and dance are other ways to strengthen this region. By giving our senses a work-out we vitalise our senses; impressions retain their life in our soul and we become much more observant.

The impulse region is the foundation

Feeling works alone in the impulse region. For example, we may have a belief in non-violence, but when punched in the nose, we fight back. It is only when we bring thinking to bear on the situation that we are able to respond in a thoughtful way. By engaging the forces of the thinking area of our soul we realise the consequences and we arrest the impulse to strike back.

The impulse region of our soul is in a dream-like state.

As we become aware of our soul's regions, and the particular activity of each region, we will experience that the impulse region with its dominant feeling levels is neither awake nor asleep. It operates in a dreamy, warm, comfortable way.

We can be mechanically subject to this region of our soul if the two higher regions are not sufficiently developed and our "I" is not sufficiently connected. A large percentage of the population have difficulty in this region. It's a "Catch 22" situation, we can be stuck here because we can't develop the other two regions and it is difficult to develop the other two because we are stuck there. The plethora of pre-packaged images served up to us by the media does not assist us to develop agility in this area of our soul.

Our irrational moments originate here.

When there is no fluidity in this region we are bound to like and dislike; objectivity can't flow in. Here are the darkest depths of our soul where we are very subject to emotions and where we find it hard to be rational and logical—which can only happen if we move up to the second, reasoning region.

An undeveloped impulse soul usually means inner emptiness, lack of inner warmth and enthusiasm, a person who is out of touch with other people and the world. These things can be overcome by encouraging imagination; building images through stories and painting images from stories.

If we think about all the images our senses are exposed to each day we can see how much traffic moves through our soul and we realise that we need a lot of energy to process it all. This explains why some people can't be bothered. We can also see why it is attractive to sit in front of the television and just let the images wash over us and not think about anything much.

Mankind developed this area of soul during Egyptian times, before Aristotle, when beauty and culture were dominant. This could mean that some people still have the soul mood of the time before Christ. Therefore what has been given to them since then lies unused or under-utilised.

This is a real possibility and through careful observation we can see it in society. It was during the time of Aristotle and at the time of Christ, that the reasoning regions were developed.

Our challenge is to become more aware of the inherent tendencies that lie in the lowest soul region and strenuously work towards a freer flowing of energy between this soul region and the next.

2. THE REASONING SOUL

What happens in the reasoning region?

Thinking arises in the rational soul.

The second region of our soul is about being rational and logical, being able to reason things through, being able to work things out. With our intelligence we can control our feelings as they arise in the impulse region of our soul and consciously manage our inclinations and desires. Our semi-conscious feelings can be awakened by our thoughts. Feeling should not be suppressed by intellect but controlled and guided by it. This is where we give things a "second thought" meaning that we add thought to the initial impulse that entered our soul, thereby balancing it.

Another word to describe this region is "harmony"—the mathematical harmony that exists when we see that two plus two equals four, or when the notes of a tune are resolved.

This is also where the ever-changing impressions, received into the first soul region from outside us, become more coherent to our inner life. Here we contemplate impressions and develop ideas and the beginnings of ideals.

Experiences in the world meet our own ideas.

In this soul region we are able to attach new external experiences to our existing internal ideas. So if we see a new person, although we do not yet know them personally, we recognise that they belong to a pattern or type of person we have already known. In this way we comprehend the continually changing outside world; it is always changing and so are we.

As the Spanish and Latin culture express the nature of the impulse soul region, the French culture is indicative of the soul mood of the second region of the human soul.

Comprehending the world

The rational region of our soul is always awake.

The activity of thinking is vital and immediate. We experience how our thoughts are awake when we compare them to our dreamy feelings. We can experience the immediacy of our thoughts when we wake up in the middle of the night, our thinking becomes active, and we cannot go back to sleep until we stop the thoughts. When we try to concentrate on one specific thought, it takes a lot of effort to keep other thoughts away.

We must strive to think energetically.

When considering the three regions of our soul we must recognise that each region has a lower and higher expression. In the lower area of this second soul region there would be an absence of original thought. There we recycle the thoughts that we receive from the outside world without testing them. These thoughts would often be abstract, theoretical concepts or even rumour. While such concepts would be accepted by people in our immediate circle, they may not stand up in a discussion with someone outside our circle.

In the lower areas of this soul region it is almost impossible to engage our "I". On the other hand, at the highest extreme of the reasoning soul, if we do not have the influence of the third, awareness soul region we can live in our highly developed theories that are only understood by others in the same, usually academic, discipline. A good example of this is when scientists say that they have the ultimate theory until another scientist puts forward a new theory. There is also a tendency for scientists to be unable to have a discussion with non-scientists. The scientist that can speak to anyone, and even explain his work in everyday terms, is the one with the highly developed I-connection and a well balanced soul.

In the rational soul the "I" emerges to purify, refine and cleanse our feelings, thoughts and actions. We need to strengthen our ability to think and to become increasingly conscious of the thoughts that flow through our mind.

Comprehension occurs in the reasoning regions of our soul.

Impressions that enter the first region of our soul, the impulse region, must move up to the reasoning regions so that we can make something of the new image. We reflect on the images and form thoughts that lead to comprehension. We compare the image with other images that we have seen in the past and we actively "try every way" (to use Aristotle's term) to understand the impression. For example, in the impulse region a glass and a cup are the same for they can both carry liquid, but in the reasoning regions we distinguish between them, finding that one has water, one has tea, one has a handle, one doesn't, one is warm, one is cold— we try every way.

Our "I" connects the thoughts that we have had in the past with the new thought caused by a new image or impression. At first this image is foreign to us. When we "try every way", we are able to harmonise the image within us and see how familiar it is when compared with similar images. The stronger our I-connection is, the sharper our thinking and the better our ability to focus our attention.

Delay judgment for as long as possible.

The second region of our soul is where we are inwardly creative; we add personal meaning to the outside impressions. We assess the value of our soul's participation in life and we work out a response to the impressions streaming in. Here we can reach some conclusion about our impressions, and then the process of judging begins. If the impulse soul is healthy our judging will be sound. If the lower soul regions are not healthy, the judging will be biased in the absence of a firm basis, a firm foundation. Whatever the result, we reach a stage where we form a concept which we deposit in our memory. It is amazing to realise that all this has transpired before we store something in our memory.

This is the part of the process that should be prolonged for as long as possible. To think a thing through, to think thoroughly about a thing, from every possible angle, to "try every way", before placing it in our memory bank assists our "I" to connect. If we do so, then our future assumptions are based on the right foundation.

It is easy to see that a thing hastily thought through and placed in our memory can be used as the basis for future misunderstandings. We might ask what kind of foundation our present perceptions stand on?

It is in this region that, when we have thought about a thing, we can then add feeling to it. In this second soul region thinking does not work alone as feeling worked alone in the first soul region. Here thinking and feeling work together and feeling is the litmus test. It tells us if a thing is right or wrong, if it rings true. This is how these soul regions work together. The best results come when the forces in the soul regions are healthy, vibrant and mobile and the I-connection is strong.

Feeling adds warmth to thinking.

Feeling adds warmth to what could otherwise be a cold, hard fact. When the outer image that impressed itself upon us (such as sound, a smell, a touch) passes to the second soul region we personalise it, we give it our own stamp of approval or disapproval. Just because the impression reaches this region does not mean that it is a good impression, worthy of our attention. It could be something unpleasant that we should have let fade and die in the first region. It is up to us whether we give life to all the images that enter us.

My new rose bush was covered in buds that would very soon blossom. I was so looking forward to the morning when I could greet my first rose. One morning I went out to see how they were doing and all that was left of the cheeky buds was the stalk that had supported them. Possums! My beautiful buds had become possum food. No matter how hard I tried I could not push my annoyance away. Why hadn't the nursery warned me? Why didn't I think of it myself? The irritation kept gnawing at me; I was keeping it alive by continuing to think about it instead of letting it go and putting it down to experience while working out how to prevent it from happening again.

What the "I" experiences in the reasoning soul

In the reasoning, logical regions of our soul there arises an affinity with the "I". The possibility of connecting with our "I" is greater because thinking is our most conscious faculty. While this region is the natural habitat of the "I" we don't become aware of the "I" until we develop the highest soul region. As previously mentioned the "I" usually doesn't have much influence in the first, impulse region of our soul. To the extent that thinking is its conscious tool, the "I" starts to see the reason behind things. The greater our understanding, the stronger our I-connection is. In this region feeling rises up to reinforce our thinking and we have a 'feeling for what is true'. It is here that thinking leads us to a feeling for what is right or not. (This is not intuition, this is logical reasoning—intuition is a different thing again which belongs to the higher spiritual regions of our being—see diagram 2.1).

All thinking, no action.

The "I" can impose itself to strongly in this soul region resulting in hard, cold intellect. Our soul can be imprisoned by the constantly revolving thoughts – often thoughts that originate from the thoughts of others, not original thoughts of our own. In this constant activity, thoughts do not lead to a conclusion or become acted upon (in the next soul region). Even when they do, the action may be unbalanced. Have you ever heard a person say something like the following?

> I have decided that I must get my life in order and do all the things that I have been putting off. I must stop doing things for others and devote all my time to myself. I must give myself and my needs priority. I have been reading a lot of books and doing a lot of soul searching and I can see how I fall short in many areas. So I am not going to do anything else for others until I do some things for myself.

This is circular reasoning. "Not doing one thing" does not ensure that another thing happens. The right outcome will occur when thinking is raised to the third, awareness region of our soul. At the awareness region we would be aware that we can achieve our personal goals while continuing to do things for others.

Although the "I" is at home in the second region of our soul, it truly comes to life in the third, awareness region. This is why there is a greater pressure on our personal development at this time in evolution; we are developing the third soul region while at the same time becoming more conscious of our "I".

Difficulties encountered in the reasoning regions

Difficulties arise because even though the "I" has its real home in this second soul region there is barely an awareness of the "I" here. It's a bit like the nose on our face which we can only see if we look in the mirror. There is a struggle in this region for the "I" to get full recognition for its ability to influence our thinking. It is only when we become more conscious in the third region of our soul that the "I" becomes more integrated and we become more conscious of it.

The "I" continually seeks to balance thinking and feeling in this region.

As we said, in this region thinking works with feeling, not just thinking alone. A thought can be very hard and cold; it will not thaw until it is warmed by feeling.

The challenge in this reasoning soul region is to be able to continually adapt. Many people can get stuck here and find anything new unpalatable. There is always the possibility of sinking back into the impulse region below and respond in a negative way to progress and change – usually because we don't make the effort to embrace possibilities through energetic thinking. If we are used to thinking with second hand thoughts, when something new approaches us, unless we use our will to actively think thoughts of our own, we have no thoughts to think.

Dangers of mechanised thinking.

If we always live on a thinking level we cannot respond to life. We would be like a washing machine stuck on one cycle: thinking, thinking, thinking. Our thinking can become quite mechanical when we operate in this region at the exclusion of the other regions, especially if we remain unconscious of the "I". An example of this mechanisation is as follows:

A father often sent his son to the hotel to buy six cans of beer. He was given five dollars and even though the cans of beer were one dollar each, he always returned with six cans of beer. One day the boy took a friend with him. As they set out his friend, who was good at mathematics said to him: 'you only have five dollars and beer costs one dollar per can, so you won't be able to buy six cans of beer; you only have enough of five'. He was being very rational about it. What he didn't know was that the custom in that hotel was that when you bought five cans of beer you got one free.

Another danger in the second soul region is that we can become very brooding; not understanding the world or showing an interest in it. The challenge is to achieve harmony of feeling in this soul region; a balance between thinking and feeling and a harmony between the inner and outer world. There must be both the input and the output to harmonise the soul-breathing. Without this soul-breathing a new idea is handled in one of two ways:

◊ our response is that "we can't see it therefore it has no value";
◊ or it is discussed endlessly but no action is taken.

Those with a static soul, whose thinking is mechanised, are unable to accept and encourage diversity. We can actually divide this region of our soul into two areas. One part is to do with our habitual mind and the other part is to do with our ability to think.

1. In the habitual mind area we can be conservative, cosy and find social convention important. Or on the other hand we can be rebellious, often objecting to things—perhaps for the sake of it—which can isolate us. If we have a tendency to one or the other we need to mix with others more widely, outside our normal social sphere. We could become more involved in our community in some way so that we extend ourselves beyond our own comfortable sphere.

2. In the thinking area we can learn to think for ourselves more often. If we fall into this group we can lack originality, or confine ourselves to a small field of interest. Or we may act automatically, or be lazy or even feel useless. If we do something different, for example, attend courses in different areas of interest or read some different books, this will broaden our outlook and at the same time give us a sense of worth. Joining a book club or interest group could be helpful.

Harmonious functioning of the reasoning soul

When we are able to achieve harmony in the second region of our soul, and when our impulse and awareness regions flow in tune with the "I", then we can 'think on our feet'.

Then we are objective, we respond intelligently and wisely in the world. What is more, we make an impression on the world that is not forgotten. These are the moments people relate back to us in later years; "I have never forgotten the time when you did such and such . . . ."

The reasoning region builds on the impulse region.

In this second soul region the "I" assimilates external impressions and quietly allows what emerges from the impulse region below to live itself out and find equilibrium. Rather than fade and die the impressions we receive gain value. Inner truth arises here. The well connected "I" can then raise this realisation to the third soul region where it becomes real and useful knowledge, wisdom in other words.

In this second region, the interplay of the forces can be observed. The soul regions should be seen as actual forces rather than a location; they have a life, they move and integrate, each coming to the fore in turn while we examine impressions, test them, apply thinking and feeling to them, until we reach a conclusion.

When an idea or impression has been processed in the reasoning regions it then moves to the third soul region, the awareness region so that we can act on our ideas. Through the development of good reasoning, our "I" will have a greater influence in the third, awareness soul region.

3. THE AWARENESS SOUL

What happens in the awareness region

Action or will arises in the awareness region of our soul.

In the third region of our soul we add awareness to our understanding. Here we find the 'aha' experience. Our thoughts are alive, active and they are our own, not second hand as they can be in the second region below. We are conscious and aware and with a strong I-connection we make wise decisions so that we act astutely in the world. This is where we become increasingly conscious of our self and our intentions in relation to our environment. When we work from this region we begin to understand the essential nature of things in a deeper way; we don't judge things superficially, we develop an awareness of what lies beneath the surface.

This is the region of wisdom.

The focus of this soul region is to reach outside into the world with the wisdom gained through the way the "I" has been able to connect in the impulse (feeling) and reasoning (thinking) regions. For a deeper understanding of this region we can also look to the characteristics of a connected "I". In this region there is less delineation between the soul and the "I" when all levels of our soul work as a team.

In terms of the evolutionary development of consciousness, this is the stage of soul development that we are working on at present. Therefore, we cannot know this region in great detail; it is a work in progress. From the fifteenth century onwards humanity began to use intellectual thinking which can lead us to completely free self-awareness. It is in this direction that we are moving as a human race and as individual human beings. Although not everyone will be at the same stage in their development as we can see from the descriptions of the other soul regions.

In fact, those who work strongly in the second soul region, especially those who have a string of tertiary qualifications for instance, often think that they are superior. There can be an élite attitude among some of these people which excludes others on the basis of tertiary achievement alone. Yet how many have produced truly original thinking? Original thinking requires an active third soul region. Excluding others through élitism is proof in itself that the "I" is not well connected.

The soul mood of the British culture reveals a lot about qualities of this third region of the soul. In contrast, we can look to the central Europeans for an understanding of the mood of the "I".

Awareness in the world

The hallmarks of this region of our soul are creativity and a moral outlook; not sexual morality, but an ability to consider the other person;

thought for others which replaces self absorption. Because this is the highest region of our soul and therefore closest to our spirit, it is in this region that we can add a spiritual perspective to our view of life—see diagram 2.1.

Awareness flows out from us like an action.

By awareness is not meant an inward awareness of self. Awareness is expressive; it flows out from us like an action. This awareness is associated with keen observation, concentration, thoughtful action, understanding, empathy and higher expressions of love.

We also become very conscious of the reasons for our actions – our motives. The more we are conscious of the reasons why we act, the more we can act in freedom. Then our faculty of will creates a force that is based on conscious motivation rather than unconscious urge. Conscious motivation belongs to the highest, most noble part of the soul; unconscious urges lack soul.

The higher our soul expressions the better we are able to strive industriously and act from our own volition. Through our own actions we earn a special kind of freedom that arises from understanding things on a deeper level. This in turn gives us courage to act where some people would not. Take this example of the difficulty in navigating a corporate environment for the health and safety of fellow workers in a large corporation.

Volunteers were asked to join the inter-state Occupational Health and Safety Committee at work. I was aware that it is very difficult to get any additional equipment and that conditions vary between staff according to how much political power the staff member has. I discovered two areas in urgent need of attention: telephone ear-phones for support calls and raised laptops so that the laptop screen is at eye level. In both cases the initial response from the committee was that it would require approval from each person's manager and cost would be a prime consideration (this is a multi-million dollar company).

We eventually got the ear phones because our office manager found some spares not being used which had been sitting in the cupboard for several years. The raised laptops took longer. I was asked to investigate the cost. I did a feasibility study and found that the equipment required would cost approximately $117 for each of the 12 members of staff. At the following meeting, the Chairman was going to pass over the subject of our laptops, "Everything's been fixed in here, hasn't it?" "No", I said. I could feel a certain hostility coming from some members of the committee, as if I had spoken out of turn. I explained how pleased the 6 people were with their earphones, and advised the approximate cost of $117.00 for a raised laptop and 12 were required. There was a rather unfriendly silence, and then fortunately a member of the committee based in interstate spoke up and said that screens at eye level were a legal requirement in there. It will be a real breakthrough when they arrive.

The person striving to improve working conditions is negotiating from a strong I-connection in the awareness soul regions. Management is responding from the unconscious self-seeking regions of the soul. They are unable to see the situation as if it affected them personally.

While we are applying the information in this book to ourselves and our friends it is also possible to apply it to modern business practices. We can translate the regions of the soul and the interaction of the "I" into corporate dynamics. The "I" can represent the CEO or the manager and those working beneath them could be arranged into teams of impulse, reasoning and awareness; and of feeling, thinking and action areas. The ideal would be that they work as a synchronised team. At a quick glance, in a corporate environment, feeling can often be overlooked—except in personal relationships between staff. Perhaps if feeling was given a more prominent role, more decisions would be made that do not disadvantage people for the sake of profit. If people take precedent over profit, profit results anyway because people usually work more conscientiously. Professionals who work in the Corporate Wellbeing industry could apply these principles in their programmes.

What the "I" experiences

Our goal is for the full unfolding of the "I" in the awareness soul region. It is in this region that the "I" experiences action in the world as meaningful and purposeful. We discover the purpose of true conscience. Conscience is about placing the other person's well-being ahead of our own, not in self sacrifice but in genuine thoughtfulness for them.

We cry the other person's tears.

Experiences can be very intense when the I-connection is strong in the awareness soul region. We can sometimes experience another's tragedy as if it happened to us. Tears may rise up when we watch the news and see the fear on a child's face, or the tears of a mother bent over her dead child. In fact, this should be our aim; that as a matter of course, we experience the pain of the person we see on the news. We are far from this point, the tragedy and terror that flash across our television screens barely touches many of us for more than a fleeting moment. Or, on the other hand, we can be over sentimental about it. We must strike the balance and experience with other person's pain objectively.

When the third region of our soul is active and vibrant there is a feeling of having found ourselves. We experience independence. We stop depending on others but at the same time work with others in a self-sustaining way.

Difficulties encountered in the awareness region

Remembering that each region has a higher and lower expression, one of our greatest difficulties in this region is that we can be very materialistic. We can also be too objective; we can keep things at arms' length and we can be too independent. We need to use our will to infuse feelings into our thoughts. When we raise ideas to this region there is a risk of becoming too scientific and too inartistic. We can express ourselves in a matter-of-fact, or even amoral, way. The lower levels of this region can be seen in a certain cunning which seeks its own advantage, where the increased level of awareness is used to take advantage of situations. The experience of power can be abused.

Agility in this region means we determine
our life instead of it determining us.

If we do not use this region of our soul to determine our life, if the events of our life are left to chance, even though our soul life is more developed than animals we can sink below the level of animals to a sub-human expression. The decline into our instincts will leave us in chaos. This is a very real experience at this stage in our development.

This means that the more highly developed our soul becomes; the lower we can fall if we are not vigilant. Responsibility resides with us. We can see such a pattern developing today in the world. Some of the most gifted people become corrupted by power. They are overcome by a feeling of invincibility. We can place the root cause of some of the world's breath-taking corporate fraud here.

It is far better to operate from the lower regions of our soul in a balanced way than to work through this region of our soul in an unbalanced way. As far as our consciousness is concerned, we must always resist the temptation to have things instantly. We don't have to force things; if we maintain our vigilant observation and do some of the exercises we will become increasingly conscious, step by step. There is an important story about this; the author is unknown.

One day, a small opening appeared in a cocoon; a man sat and watched for several hours for a butterfly to appear. It struggled to force its body through that little hole. Then, it seems to stop making any progress. It appeared as if it had reached as far as it could and it could not go any further. So the man decided to help the butterfly: he took a pair of scissors and opened the cocoon. The butterfly then emerged easily.

But it had a withered body, it was tiny with shrivelled wings.

The man continued to watch because he expected that, at any moment, the wings would open, enlarge and expand, to be able to support the butterfly's body, and become firm. Neither happened! In fact, the butterfly spent the rest of its life crawling around with a withered body and shrivelled wings. It never was able to fly.

What the man, in his kindness and his goodwill, did not understand was that the restricting cocoon and the struggle required for the butterfly to get through the tiny opening, were nature's way of forcing fluid from the body of the butterfly into its wings, so that it would be ready for flight once it achieved its freedom from the cocoon.

The awareness region must work harmoniously with the reasoning and impulse regions of our soul

It requires a lot of courage and confidence to operate out of the awareness soul regions because here we are breaking new ground. We work with unknowns like the birth of the butterfly from its cocoon. A new and different expression comes to life from this soul region and this may not sit well in the accepted culture of today.

When we experience the strength and wisdom of this part of our soul we lose our awkward self-consciousness and we overcome the inhibitions which prevent us from expressing our self in a more complete way. We are confident but not overly confident. We have a self-assurance which needs no specific expression, it is self-evident. We can confuse these expressions of the highest soul region with the egotism of the pseudo-self. It requires a strong I-connection to tell the difference.

When we express ourselves harmoniously through the three regions of our soul we begin to have a greater sense of community. Not community in a tribal sense, it is more about taking responsibility for our own actions knowing that whatever we do creates the world we live in.

Thinking, feeling and willing can be more co-operative in the awareness region.

In the third region of our soul the tools of the "I", willing, thinking and feeling, operate as a more cohesive team. We are also able to have more control of them. The more developed the third region of our soul is, the more easily we can use one or the other, or any combination, to the greatest effect in our life.

As this is the highest region of our soul it is here that we approach the human spirit. In its natural state the awareness region of our soul is unconscious or asleep—unaware. If we can awaken this region, make it active, we will experience various states of self knowledge and self awareness. This self awareness is accompanied by an increased awareness of the world outside. We are more aware of others and how they are expressing themselves through their "I" and soul. This level of awareness is not always comfortable; we may see more than we bargained for. To have insight into other people and their motivations can be difficult and it can certainly shock us. Therefore we need a strong I-connection which gives us a greater level of understanding and forgiveness.

The process of self-knowledge is on-going and through our understanding of the different soul regions we can trace this development. Each one of us will experience this awakening in a different way because we each have a different soul constitution and soul mood. We are each influenced differently by our place of birth, our family and upbringing, our friends, our occupation and so on; these are the things that colour our soul.

The awareness soul region is a work in progress.

The hallmarks of a healthy awareness soul region are unselfishness, tolerance and the ability to see the positive side of things. Hindrances in this area which arise out of the lower levels of this soul region are to do with having a materialistic greed, uninhibited sexuality, being power hungry or money hungry, escaping through the use of drugs, reviving outmoded spirituality and glorifying sporting professionals beyond an appropriate level. All of these expressions are firmly imbedded in society today. While we can be critical of these tendencies in society, we must also acknowledge that they also indicate that the highest soul regions are awakening in many people. Since the highest soul regions are also associated with free will each person is responsible for the choices they make. When we deal with the will we must always ensure that we do not impose our will on others, or let them impose their will on us.

As we develop our third soul region we must work hard to develop ethical judgements for our actions. How will our actions affect others? The effort required, in other words, the amount of will required, often deters us from thinking things through thoroughly enough to see beyond our own needs.

This soul region will awaken if we enter deeply into the experiences of life. One of the life experiences that has been ignored for so long, but which we are beginning to enter into more, is death. People who have had a narrow escape from death always say that they no longer fear death. To think more deeply about such things will increase our awareness and strengthen the third region of our soul.

We know that we are strengthened when we have new experiences. Stretching our boundaries is a pre-requisite for developing our soul to its full potential. We need to be daring and step outside the boundaries of life-long patterns. The more we can embrace that which is foreign to us, the more enlivened and versatile our soul will be and the more connected we are with our "I".

Soul development within different cultures and regions of the world

Just as history reveals the changing consciousness of humanity, so we are able to see how different countries align with the different soul regions. As pointed out earlier, the French have the mood of the second region of the soul, Spanish or Latin cultures have the mood of the first region and the British express the nature of the third soul region. It is obvious that certain nations have been more influential than others throughout history and this points to development of the soul and the "I".

Higher soul development unites people.

One of the benefits of the number of people migrating around the world, especially since World War II, is that the soul moods of the different countries merge. This is in line with the individual development of the soul when, in the third region, the different soul regions work together in harmony.

We can certainly see the struggle towards this global swing today in the world. Those who want to express themselves from the fundamental principles of their own religion or region try to impose their will in terrifying ways on those who are developing their consciousness at the forefront of evolution. Of course, many people in the western world are also not expressing themselves at the highest levels of consciousness. We see this in materialistic objectivity, in greed, scientific modification of plants, animals and even humans in the form of cloning. We also see an amoral matter-of-factness, as well as degraded sexuality. We need to wake up to the fact that humanity is going through a transition of consciousness, and like a child learning to walk we will often fall until we are very steady on our feet.

To avoid being too prescriptive in this book, a personal exploration of the different cultures will identify the soul mood that prevails there. By saying that the British people reveal the essence of the awareness soul, don't accept it but look to their culture for clues of it. In Britain we can see tradition standing in opposition to the new impulses of soul development and I-connection. The transition to strengthen the third soul region is threatened by our bondage to outer things, to materialistic views of the world instead of an inner understanding of the human soul and spirit.

Instead of moving forward with the forces of this soul region we are trying to drag the forces of the rational, logical soul into the present. The catch cry is "Through intellect we can understand not through awareness!" The inclinations of ancient Greece and Rome are tugging us back; the new impulses of the awareness soul region make many of us uncomfortable. Science says, "No, the intellect must understand, we cannot have an unsupported thought come into our mind. Six cans of beer costs six dollars, there is no way we can get six cans of beer for five dollars."

The German's have the mood of the "I". Look to the German culture to understand the characteristics of the "I". In the Russian culture we can see developing the first regions of the spirit, the level above the soul—see diagram 2.1. Obviously we can't take one German and one Russian as an example; we must look at the whole culture, their history and the mood of the people; we can even look for it in their facial features.

When we recognise the different soul moods in the different societies around the world we see racial discrimination in a different light. We could then say that this kind of discrimination occurs in those people who live in the lower soul regions, they find those who have developed their higher soul regions foreign or even threatening. We can identify many different soul characteristics in the various cultures, for example, Hungarians like to be sad, Italians like to be happy. If we look closely into these things we will discover many secrets of the soul.

Eastern cultures have a totally different sense of the "I"—it is as if they cannot relate to an "I" within them but that it always accompanies them like an outer spiritual deity. Close observation shows that world migration gives people the opportunity to experience, and often merge, the different expressions of the "I" and soul.

Self-knowledge though our I-connection

As we work inwardly on our self and our soul processes, the "I" becomes more conscious of itself. Outwardly, from an historical point of view we can trace this development and refinement of the soul and the "I". From these two perspectives we can have a better understanding of world events as well as of human development.

True self knowledge is to experience the ebb and flow of the constructive and destructive forces which move between our conscious mind and that which our mind is not conscious of; to become aware of them. That is the reason for calling the third soul region the awareness region. Self knowledge is not about discovering what we have unconsciously deposited in the subconscious mind; self knowledge is about being conscious. The more conscious we become the less there can be in our so-called subconscious mind!

Disharmony, dislike, and hatred are destructive for our soul.

As our self knowledge increases we understand how we can use our I-connection to kindle harmony and peace within us and around us. The "I" doesn't like or dislike; it balances, neutralises and understands opposing views. As we become more conscious, the light of our "I" shines from within our soul. The "I" is like a fire which burns more brightly when we fuel it with our conscious life. The more conscious we are the more involvement our "I" has with our soul. Over time, the elements of soul and spirit become increasingly independent and the influence of the body does not eclipse the influence the "I".

While our "I" lives in our feeling, thinking and willing, it should not be too closely entwined in these activities for then the "I" cannot retain its objectivity. Thinking, feeling and willing enable us to solve life's problems and to develop inner strength as well as to invigorate our soul for outer action. Therefore the I-connection must be tweaked so that we can be mobile and flexible to respond to the demands of modern life in a controlled and conscious way.

The "I" is active not passive.

When our highest soul region awakens we become very aware of how the "I" is the active principle in our life through which we take control of our life. The "I" expresses itself in knowledge (wisdom not intellect) and judging. The "I" does not statically 'sit in judgment' but is itself involved in a continual act of judging. Judging is a continual series of adjustments; these adjustments give us an experience of justice. When we have engaged with our "I" in the right way we experience a continual discerning, and in this way we can easily make life's decisions. We can direct our attention to wherever it is needed and change our focus as often as needed.

Also, the more our "I" has the right relationship with our body and soul the more we value truth, goodness and beauty. Our values can change dramatically. An inner response of awe for other people, the miracle of life and the creativity of the human being grows within us. We begin to become attentive to the finest detail in situations around us. We act with wisdom and warmth, compassion and love. We increasingly come to understand how powerful the "I" can be. It is like fire—it can warm or it can burn.

Awaken the sleeping forces of our soul.

Once we begin to awaken the sleeping forces in our soul we set up a momentum, but not a momentum of inertia that rolls forward undirected, of its own volition, like a rolling stone. We engage with this momentum and ride the dislodged rock that is our soul, guiding its path to a planned destination.

There is an ancient exercise that has been handed down the centuries. It strengthens our thinking and our will and assists us to engage our "I" in the awareness region of our soul.

Focus your attention on a pencil or any simple object you choose. Close your eyes, relax your body and see the image of the pencil in your mind. Concentrate on the pencil, think of nothing but the pencil. Think of the lead, the wood, the lacquer. Does it have a rubber? Does it have words printed on the side? Is it beautiful? How is it manufactured? Find out everything about pencils; the 'lead' pencil (which contains not lead but graphite) was invented in 1564 when graphite was discovered in Cumbria, England (the time which coincides with the beginning of the development of the awareness soul regions). While you are holding the image, imagine it as a functioning object. See it writing and connect up with the idea of 'pencil'. Maintain your concentration on the pencil and every time another thought unrelated to pencils tries to enter your mind use your will focus your attention on the pencil again. Try to do this for a few minutes each day until eventually you can stay focussed on the pencil for at least 10 minutes. Then try it with something simpler like a pin or a needle.

After the exercise we must think about how we used our will to think about the pencil. We find that we think about the pencil for a while when another thought intrudes, for example, 'I really need to take the dog for a walk'. At this point we have to engage our will by directing our thinking back to the pencil, as well as to stay with the image of the pencil. The point is not about staying continually with the pencil, but about experiencing the strength of will that it takes to keep other thoughts out. When we experience the will in this way we become aware of the force of our "I" directing our will. We also experience how the "I" brings order into our soul, into our feeling, thinking and willing which can otherwise be disorderly or automatic. Then our "I" has the opportunity of becoming aware of itself. The more we do this exercise the more we become conscious of the faculties in our soul. Then we can use it consciously to stay focussed and concentrate better on our daily tasks. In this way we involve our "I" more often in our life in a conscious way.

This simple exercise reveals the nature of the partnership between our soul and our "I" and can assist us to see how our inner self communicates with the world around us. Kahlil Gibran in "The Prophet" speaks clearly about the partnership of our soul and our "I" and gives clear guidance for the harmonious development of all the soul regions.

Speak to us of reason and passion

And he answered, saying:

Your soul is oftentimes a battlefield, upon which your reason[1] and your judgment[2] wage war against your passion and your appetite[3].

Would that I could be the peacemaker in your soul, that I might turn the discord and the rivalry of your elements into one-ness and melody.

But how shall I, unless you yourselves be also the peacemakers, nay, the lovers of all your elements?

Your reason and your passion are the rudder and the sails of your seafaring soul.

If either your sails or your rudder be broken, you can but toss and drift, or else be held at a standstill in mid-seas.

For reason, ruling alone, is a force confining; and passion, unattended, is a flame that burns to its own destruction.

Therefore let your soul exalt your reason to the height of passion, that it may sing;

And let it direct your passion with reason, that your passion may live through its own daily resurrection, and like the phoenix rise above its own ashes.

I would have you consider your judgment and your appetite even as you would two loved guests in your house.

Surely you would not honour one guest above the other; for he who is more mindful of one loses the love and the faith of both.

—KAHLIL GIBRAN *The Prophet*

FOOTNOTES

1 reason represents the second region of the soul and thinking
2 judgment represents the third region and our will
3 passion and appetite live in the first soul region and feeling

Chapter 5: Healthy Soul, Strong I-Connection: exercises

Our journey so far has given us a detailed picture of our soul and its three regions, and how our "I" expresses itself through feeling, thinking and willing in our soul and our body to interact with our environment. The stronger the I-connection the more conscious and purposeful these interactions will be.

We have also seen how the soul and the I-connection have developed throughout history and that this development has been focussed in certain countries throughout the world. It would be an interesting study to link this to the power of nations and their economic development.

We have experienced how our "I" is actually the eye of our being. By now we should have some idea of how blind we can be if our soul obscures the "I" by expressing its habitual patterns. Our "I" can 'see' to the extent that our soul is awake and connected with our "I". The more we 'see' the more conscious we become and the healthier we are on all the levels of our being; body, soul and spirit.

When we become more conscious we have more choice in our life and hence more freedom. The beginnings of freedom can be as simple as the awareness of choices. The urge to freedom is inherent in our being and restlessness is often its birth pangs. How we apply our will to direct this restlessness and, in turn, how we express freedom is pivotal to the health of our soul. An important step is to become more aware of the subtle way we use our will. Do we try to influence others by imposing our will on them? This can be as simple as trying to convince others of our own view of things. Or do we express ourselves as individuals in community with other individuals? The greatest test for this is how strongly we cling to our own ideas without remaining open to the ideas of others, and whether our own ideas evolve or stay the same.

The quest of the soul is to know self and to know others.

As we experience the work of our soul and our "I" within our being we realise that there is much more to know about ourselves than we know at present. This is the quest of the soul; to become conscious enough to know self and to know others. This quest is not particularly arduous; it is simply a journey of increasing awareness, of becoming more conscious day by day. The pace of the quest is completely optional and each step changes us forever. If we awaken our soul it will never sleep again. Once a flower blooms it cannot un-bloom! If we are determined to engage more fully with our "I" then our I-connection matures and influences our life henceforth.

This does not mean that we will not be diverted from our quest. We may be satisfied with our initial results. We always have the freedom to work on our soul and "I" or not. However, once our soul comes to life we are more able to continue the quest. A natural momentum can build which assists us to ride the wave of conscious soul awareness and I-connectedness. For many, it is a relief that this method of self-development is not a struggle but rather becomes a natural part of life.

Our soul, as we have seen, prefers to be in a state of rest. It is stirred into action either by an *external influence* or through our *own effort*. Generally an external influence will override our own effort. If we continually allow external influences to activate our soul, especially the will of another person, our soul forces can be diluted. By keeping our soul awake and alert, by preventing it from spending too much time in its native dream-state, we will be less influenced by others and less influenced by our own unconscious past memories. A small amount of self knowledge will motivate us to continue taking more steps towards being more self aware.

Challenges to overcome if our "I" is to express itself through our soul

The health of our soul is based on the wisdom of inner experience, not theory.

We need a healthy, active and alive soul so that our "I" can gain experience through it. If we don't have an active soul, our "I" doesn't have a complete experience of the world; without "I" and soul engaged, our body is reduced to a sensory apparatus. We don't allow the world to enter into us and so we are not experiencing life as fully as we could.

How healthy is our soul and how do we know? We cannot assess the forces and functions of the soul as a spectator, or rely on the diagnosis of others, but only through our conscious participation in the soul's activities. We must have a living understanding of our own soul, from the inside, not as an onlooker. Test this out by thinking about how hard it is to describe a feeling such as happiness or sadness. To understand a feeling we must experience a feeling. Another person may only experience a feeling that we have had if we can find a way to assist them to feel it too.

Likewise, the health of our soul is based on the wisdom of inner experience, not theory and facts. We try to become more conscious of how we traverse the spectrum of consciousness within our soul through-out the day; from unconscious, semi-conscious, conscious, self-conscious, to super-conscious. We cannot learn this working of our soul from a description or explanation, but only from a direct experience. The Quest of the Soul Workshop and Workbook are designed with this in mind. They assist us to have a firsthand experience of our soul and our "I".

When our soul begins to come alive within us, and when we become conscious of the activities of our soul and "I", this has an immediate affect on our character and our personality.

Character is the result of the harmony
or disharmony experienced by our "I".

Remember the picture of the "I" as the musician playing the three stringed instrument of the soul. We live in the 'music' that the "I" creates in our soul. Can our being dance to the music or does it want to 'sit this one out'? Do we dance through life taking the lead or are we always running to catch up and stepping on a few toes?

Our challenge is to work with the activity of the soul and to resist the natural inclination towards inactivity. Not only that, as we succeed in this process we have to meet the challenges that arise as the new partnership between our soul and "I" develops.

Many people associate their soul with their heart. Indeed, the centre of the soul is found in the heart and the heart and the blood are also the focal point for the "I", the self. Increasingly today we hear that we must try to think with our heart. This does not mean that we should be led by our feelings; it means that we should combine the head and the heart, thinking and feeling as we described in the last chapter when discussing the reasoning soul region. This is the sign that our "I" and our soul are creating a new partnership. The challenge is to combine the two, neither to emphasise feeling, nor to emphasise thinking but to create harmony between them.

While we set our goals for our quest we should be very aware that there are obstacles. Because our quest takes place in the real world, these obstacles can be twofold. The first one can be found in society itself. The modern world, which is influenced so strongly by governments who focus on economic policy, actually works against our soul-I development. The second one is that we can be our own obstacle.

The modern world makes our soul sick

General observation reveals the amount of soul-sickness in the world. The "I" cannot associate with a sick soul. The "I" can only engage with a vibrant and active soul. We have touched on some of the things that create these soul-sicknesses: The emptiness and irrelevance of statistics, the lack of energy in a soul that is fed prepared images through the media, and the isolation experienced through an unsatisfactory social life - these are among the enemies of the soul. We can identify different soul illnesses which make our soul weak, lifeless and dull and relate them to the activity of the forces of feeling, thinking and willing.

The world can be soul-numbing.

The media has an agenda which seeks to influence us, not for our own benefit but for their financial gain. They confuse our thinking when we are presented with 'cold hard facts'. These 'facts', disconnected as they are from the warmth of feeling, cannot call forth action. What are we to do with, or even feel about, the 'fact' that .02% of people get headaches from eating chocolate? Using statistics to make decisions is no different to gambling. Gambling terminology is even used. If 50% of people die at the age of 80 what odds does that give us for living till the age of 80? What do we do with this information? Worry? Spend time planning our life instead of living it? This meaningless information crystallises the soul!

For a full understanding of our being we must continually remind ourselves that we perceive the world through our body's senses; we experience the world through the soul and we understand the world through our spirit, through our "I". It is a team effort. Statistics or 'facts' relate to our physical existence in the world and they say little or nothing about our soul or spirit. They do not even necessarily tell us what is actually possible in the physical world, for example, that it is possible to buy six cans of beer for the price of five. Statistics only relate to physical perception; they cannot lead to an experience or full understanding of human life.

Such lifelessness of soul cannot assist our "I" to distinguish between what is good and what is bad. When we listen to too many rational arguments or 'facts', our ability to know what is right actually diminishes and we experience uncertainty. This is not just information overload, it is soul destroying.

Soul destroying processes can be found everywhere in modern society. Look at the amount of choice we are given when we buy a mobile phone, take out a mortgage or even simply shop for groceries. The wiring in our soul short circuits and we are tempted not to make a choice at all. This process actually prevents our second soul region from becoming active so that we are unable to apply reason to the situation. Mobile phone plans are a magical delusion which foil our I-connection and dull our soul.

There are three major areas of soul sickness.

I. DULLNESS OF SOUL AFFECTS OUR WILL

We experience this when we:

◊ are dissatisfied;

◊ do not or cannot actively think things through, which makes us unconscious;

◊ can't relate to the world as something we create through our own actions;

◊ have little hope for the future.

Like a brass statue that is not polished our soul can lose its brilliance though neglect. This dullness pervades life and we can experience a dampening or 'dumbing-down' of our experience of life. Our will dominates without the support of thinking. We may protest from a one-sided point of view, possibly protesting for protest's sake. We move through life in an unconscious way. The following news story highlights just how unconscious we can be even when we have taken on the responsibility of caring for someone else's child.

> A child-care centre is being investigated by the Government after a 14-month-old boy was left locked inside when staff left for the day. The baby's mother arrived late at the childcare centre and found the main door locked and no staff inside. The frantic woman used her mobile phone to call police. "She was hysterical," the police said. The woman asked a gardener working nearby and a neighbour to help and they were about to break into the building when they found a back door was unlocked. By the time police arrived, the woman had recovered her baby son, who was unharmed and had slept through the drama.

When our soul is dull our work is seen as a means to end, we are not motivated to do our best when, by doing the minimum, we still earn our money at the end of the day. The lack of consciousness means that our soul and our heart are not in our work. This is deadly for us and deadly for the world.

2. LIFELESSNESS OF SOUL AFFECTS OUR THINKING

There is no life in our soul when we are brooding within ourselves. We are captured within our soul, locked in the second soul region in the domain of thinking, logic and reason. This thinking becomes isolated from feeling and willing and has no life, no warmth in it, and its focus is narrow. The breathing action of the soul is restrained, as if we are holding our breath, and in this lack of movement our soul stagnates. Examples of this are found in people who study a narrow field of knowledge at the exclusion of all others. Or those who indulge in activities of escapism, lack self-creativity, live their life through habitual patterns. The personality can be monotonous, the feelings rarely expressed and actions are sluggish.

Lifelessness of soul can also arise in those who wallow in the lower regions of their soul. They continually take in stimulus from the outside world without engaging with the impulses that approach them because it is too much effort. They are inclined to live their life through television, movies, magazines and gossip: other people's reality.

3. WEAKNESS OF SOUL AFFECTS OUR FEELING

Apart from being dull or lifeless our soul can also be weak. We can turn away from the new in an act of *self preservation*. This happens when we instinctively feel that we would be thrown into confusion if we opened ourselves to anything new that approaches us. However, clinging to the past gives us a false sense of security.

Alternatively, we can become mindlessly addicted to the new, taking in more and more without understanding it, without testing it with reason and logic, until we drown. This is *self annihilation*. We race into a hastily prepared future. Weakness of soul points to feelings which dominate and displace thinking and willing.

The healthy soul must manage the interaction of feeling, thinking and willing so that each one comes to the fore, supported by the others, at appropriate times. This is orchestrated by a strong I-connection.

There are many ways to strengthen and energise our soul regions so that our "I" can have a greater influence in our lives. In addition to the ongoing work of recognising which soul regions and soul faculties we are expressing, we can also identify specific areas that require strengthening and give them a work out. This chapter suggests some practical exercises that can be easily integrated into daily life. Some exercises affect our inner life; others affect the way we relate to the world around us.

When we are conscious of our soul's activities,
we know what activities are best for its development.

Once we recognise how often our soul dreams its life away in a warm sea of feelings, we can also become conscious of what wakes it up. Awake and alert our soul will assist us to *respond* thoughtfully to situations that life presents instead of *reacting* instinctively. A conscious response makes us feel sronger, more confident, and more peaceful.

Through this awareness of how we feel, think and act, our "I" has a more immediate influence in our soul and we can be more objective more frequently. For instance, if someone criticises us we will easily be able to see why they say what they do. This new information then assists us to make adjustments if necessary. When we have a strong I-connection we will also be able to stand by our actions even if others do not appreciate or understand them.

Healing for the soul

There are many ways to bring healing to our soul. When this healing occurs there are two main outcomes:

1. Enlivening the soul and strengthening the I-connection to the point of being able to naturally and easily distinguish between good and bad, right and wrong.
2. Enlivening the soul so that we can know self objectively.

This also summarises the main issues facing modern society. Anyone wishing to have a better understanding of the cause of many modern illnesses would find this a fruitful place to begin the search.

As we have said, the "I" is independent and individual. The word individual means undivided, complete, whole. Individuality has taken on a different meaning today which can be more about selfishness than wholeness.

We know that the "I", as the self-conscious kernel of the human soul, must gain experience of the world through the soul. If the soul is dull, lifeless or weak this becomes an impossible task. Therefore healing must start with our soul.

Strengthening feeling, thinking and willing fills the soul with life.

We must find as many ways as possible for giving our soul a work-out. As our soul becomes more energetic it is strengthened to embrace the future. Our feeling, thinking and willing are renewed and the work-out continues as we get used to the new way they operate. For this we require the judging ability and intelligence that we acquire through our I-connection.

Embracing the future means that we move away from our old position actively and willingly. We can't sit in our old position while trying to see if the new is worth budging for. This activity of experiencing the new has a strengthening quality to it. We can best achieve this by balancing our work in the world with our work on self. Like the rhythmic inhaling and exhaling of breath, the world is taken in, we change, and then we act in the world in new ways. We must apply our inner forces to handle the outside world and from the outside world we draw strength for a healthy inner life. The two go hand in hand. This is 'soul breathing'. Then the soul, which is situated between the body and the spirit, masters the body and responds to the spirit.

Another key component of the awakened soul is to be observant and aware; to notice what is in the world so that we receive vivid impressions into our soul. For this we have to let the world touch us and overcome the instinct to withdraw.

When our "I" and soul activities become more conscious, then, in a compound way, the "I" can incite the soul regions to greater activity and a more measured response. When we react to criticism, for instance, our "I" remains in the background and its influence is weak. To ensure our whole being is healthy and active we can work-out in the soul gym regularly.

The soul gym

What does a soul workout look like? It is not that dissimilar to training our body. It is well known that our physical body has a memory of its own. Musicians, dancers, sports professionals and touch typists are among those who recognise that their actions are made possible through body or muscle memory. It is not possible to consciously direct large sets of complex physical tasks consciously; some of them have to be practised and performed unconsciously. As we have been discovering, our soul also works unconsciously.

To put this into perspective we need to differentiate between the work of the will in the soul and in the body. The unconscious actions of the will in our body direct practised movement and also other movements like our metabolism, digestion and circulation. Imagine what it would be like having to consciously digest every meal we ate or to remember to take a breath every few seconds. While the unconscious will is a good thing for the body, it is not so good for the soul. The body on autopilot keeps us alive, the soul on autopilot means our consciousness is dull.

If we want to be physically fit, we go to the gym and undertake prescribed physical movements. In the same way, if we want our soul to be strong and flexible in its response to life we need to flex its 'muscles'. Our soul will not automatically become supple and compliant; we need to use our will to achieve this. As we have seen our soul seeks comfort and rest and the pleasure of old patterns.

1. FIRST WE MUST BECOME AWARE OF OUR SOUL AND "I"

The previous chapters have equipped us to become aware of some of the activity of our soul and our "I". However, it remains that we have grown up focussing on our body and to place more emphasis on our soul and spirit means we have to break some old habits.

We develop our soul through becoming conscious of its activities.

So it is not a simple matter of being told that we have a soul; it is entirely up to each of us to give our soul its rightful place within our being. We can only do this when we recognise how we feel, think and will and how these soul faculties interact with each other. We explored these faculties in some detail in chapter 3.

One of the first things we need to do is to become aware of which soul regions we use the most. If we are a feeling person then we need to try to add thoughts to our feelings as often as possible, always remembering that feelings cannot be changed; they can only be guided. If we are a thinking person then we must seek every opportunity to allow feeling to warm our thoughts. We need also to become aware of the nature of our thoughts. We can only transform our thinking through concentration which requires the use of our will. We need to become more aware of the role will plays in our soul life. How strong is our will? How do we apply it? We can only transform our will through meditation.

Remember that it is our "I" which feels, thinks and wills in our soul. If our feeling, thinking and willing function automatically then our I-connection is weak. Our soul uses our body to express these feelings, thoughts and actions. Our soul has enough learned responses to carry on with life automatically but at this stage in evolution our "I" is demanding a more prominent place in our soul. While we remain unconscious of the activities of our "I" in our soul we experience the "I" as an unknown pressure. This pressure causes anxiety that some people are inclined to relieve with stimulants like alcohol, drugs, computer games and gambling.

The strength to deal with a situation comes from our awakened soul and our "I".

If we approach the world only from a physical perspective, if we do not let our soul and our "I" take their rightful place, we will struggle to handle demanding situations by ourselves. This is of increasing concern when more people are opting not to marry or form close relationships. The number of news reports of the deaths of elderly people not being discovered, even months after they have died, is alarming.

The more conscious we are of our total being, the more likely we are to form relationships with others in our community and the less dependent we will be on the support of others. We will have strength of character and good moral fibre, with an active conscience and a peaceful disposition.

It is worth noting that peace is a very misunderstood word. To experience peace is not to be free of difficulties, but rather to be able to deal with difficulties graciously. To be peaceful is not about being timid; it is about being quietly confident with a strong I-connection to take in our stride whatever comes our way.

2. WORKING CONSCIOUSLY WITH THE POLARITIES IN OUR SOUL

The second step in the soul gym is to look closely at what takes place in our soul. One of the first things we notice is the opposite experiences we have, especially with dominant feelings like love and hate. We have already discussed this in some detail in chapter 3 when we looked at the life cycle of the soul. It is helpful to observe how often during the day we love or hate. How often do we hear people say, "I love that" or "I hate that"? We even avoid using the word hate, thinking we soften the experience by using words like dislike or "that is not my preference". The fact remains that the core feelings in our soul are love and hate.

Another challenge comes from the essential tone of the soul which leans towards things which are unifying rather than dividing. The soul continually seeks the path of least resistance. It will deal with differences in two ways; either to build a bridge through love or to destroy the bridge through hate. It is helpful to be aware that the soul in its natural state can be quite primitive. Through a strong I-connection we stay with the experiences of love and hate without trying to minimise them. Then we can balance these feelings and raise them up to a level where we can co-exist with differences. The "I" gives us the objectivity to do this.

Consider the following responses and reactions of a person trying to find a space to park a car:

> As I was driving around the car park, a person thoughtfully signalled that they were about to vacate their spot. I felt a warmth and understanding flow between us. Just as I was pulling into the vacant spot another person tried to take it, and anger roared up in me. I felt hate for this person who was cheating me out of my parking space. It shocked me to experience the hate for the person and the possessiveness of the space. At that moment, I saw that the person wanting to take the spot was disabled and had no other place to park so close to the entry to the mall. I let them have the parking space. It was an unsettling experience to flow from gratitude to anger to hate to compassion in seconds. It was then that I came to an understanding of how very close the relationship was between anger and love.

The above example demonstrates that life is not so much a series of events as a continual engagement with the forces within us and around us. The forces of love and hate are continually flowing and weaving within us and through our "I" we can keep them in balance and our responses will be measured.

The first thing we have to do is understand how the opposing experiences fill our soul. Without understanding one polarity, we cannot fully experience the other. For example, without experiencing the depths of sorrow we cannot know the heights of joy. It is the experience of both sorrow and joy that assists us to find a balance between these two opposites. The greater harmony can only be achieved by passing through disharmony.

> I was invited to the beach for the weekend with a group of people. My initial response to the invitation was that it would be really interesting and exciting and worthwhile. As the time drew near my initial interest was replaced by uncertainty. I thought: I will not be accepted, worse, I

will be rejected, I won't fit in and will want to leave before the end of the weekend. Perhaps I won't go at all. So I sat down and visualized the weekend, 'feeling' the presence of each person who was going to be present, realizing my connection with each person and the spiritual bond and love between us; that it will be okay.

We can see how the I-connection balanced the polarities. This is how we raise ourselves above the polarity to create harmony in our being. If we are going to spend time with others, at work or elsewhere, our I-connection assists us not to be swayed one way or the other. Our relationships will be more successful and we can come to love people more readily while accepting what causes distress or annoyance about them.

These are some of the polarities that are experienced by our soul. If is useful for us to take some time to remember moments in our life when we have experienced these opposites. To what extent did we let ourselves experience the extremes, and to what extent were we able to rise above them to a higher balanced expression?

Acceptance	Rejection
Attachment	Detachment
Attraction	Repulsion
Bright	Dull
Confidence	Low self esteem
Elation	Depression
Exaggeration	Understatement
Harmony	Discord
Hope	Fear
Independence	Dependence
Joy	Sorrow
Life	Death
Losing self in self	Losing self in others/environment
Love	Hate
Pain	Compassion
Unity	Diversity
Useful	Harmful

In most cases when one or the other dominates, balance is lost in our soul. Only our I-connection can restore the balance through harmonising feeling, thinking and willing. To experience the extremities of these opposites takes courage, we are usually more comfortable in the middle ground where we don't experience them fully. Our soul-I relationship will suffer if we deny the spectrum of experience. For instance, how can we fully experience life if we have no experience of death? We can't ignore all the stories written about how much more meaningful life is to the one who has a brush with death. We need a strong I-connection to elevate us above the middle ground and experience these extremities which can be a very magnetic experience in the soul. We have to break through the magnetism and rise above it.

Testing these processes in our life as frequently as possible will make us conscious of what transpires within our own being. The right responses will become second nature through the careful observation of our experiences.

Exercise

Sit quietly and think about how you lose yourself in yourself. Then switch to contemplating how you lose yourself in others or in your environment. Then try to envisage a new way of being where you exist in your environment and you don't 'lose' yourself but find your creative place. You will experience a confident ebb and flow between yourself and others.

We are individuals in our soul expression.

It is helpful to think about how we relate to our different friends and acquaintances. Are we protective with some, more trusting with others? In some friendships tension can arise when we want to be swallowed up by our friend, we let them make all the decisions about where we go and what we do. This can become a burden for them. Or we can dominate and always want things to go our way. Instead we can stand in our I-connection and discuss preferences and reach good decisions with some give and take. It is wonderful to be able to develop a healthy respect for each other as individuals and have the freedom to express ourselves differently.

3. RECOGNISE THE SOUL BLIND-SPOTS

When we observe our soul more closely we come to know that as we move through our day our soul is often not consciously involved in what we are doing. To become aware of times when our soul has not been active, we can take note of the next time we do something and do not remember the steps we took. During that blank period of time, our body performed the tasks automatically and our soul forces were completely by-passed. There was a blind spot in our soul.

The other day when I was putting on my makeup and I pulled out a drawer to get my mascara. Because I wasn't concentrating, I pulled out the wrong drawer. As I looked into it and didn't see my mascara (which would have jogged my memory) I just didn't know what to make of what I was looking at. Finally, I was able to jolt myself out of my automatic action and induce my thinking and make sense of what I was looking at.

When our automatic processes take over, our soul faculties are resting. An impression enters, we don't know what to make of it and so we try to engage the reasoning regions of our soul to make more sense of things. Only when our thinking is stirred can we connect things we know (from the past) with a new piece of information that we have just received.

Life is full of examples if we notice them.

Interestingly, our language reflects this. For example, when a person forgets to do something they will say, 'it didn't cross my mind' or 'I didn't think'. The sense impression stayed in the first, impulse soul region where it faded and died before it could make it up to the second, reasoning region which we associate with our mind.

We can see how our body can act automatically excluding our soul and, also, our soul can act automatically excluding our "I". We can become more conscious of how this happens by changing some of our habits.

Exercise

Do we fasten our seatbelt after we have started driving down the road? We do this automatically without thinking. We can make a conscious decision to fasten our seatbelt before we put the keys in the ignition. This is one way to make the physical processes in our body more conscious.

When it comes to our automatic soul processes that exclude the "I", we must look at our automatic feeling, thinking or actions. Do we get angry each time the neighbour's dog barks? We can't do anything about it so why not replace the anger with another response. We could sing or we could simply block out the sound by concentrating on something else.

4. FOSTERING THE TEAMWORK OF OUR SOUL AND "I"

An inner sense of right and wrong
develops from a strong soul-I connection.

When we have worked on our soul for a while we become aware of when it is lively and when it rests. At the same time we can be more conscious of our I-connection. This assists us to determine right from wrong so that decisions can be made more easily. This gives us a feeling of freedom because we can act on our feet without being too ponderous or seeking other opinions.

> I was waiting to be interviewed for a job. Waiting with me was another applicant my age. We got talking and the other boy asked me if I was really nervous too. I wasn't so I asked him why he was so nervous. The boy replied that he had no idea what questions they might ask and what answers he should give—would they want the conservative answer or a more cutting edge response, what viewpoint would they be coming from? I told him that I knew that all the answers I needed to give were within me. I suggested that all he had to do was be himself.

When our soul is full of life we can speak with confidence from our "I" and express who we really are without seeking approval. Others will usually respond favourably to us because our honesty attracts respect. Differences are viewed differently.

It is possible for our "I" to develop independently of the soul. This causes an intensity of the "I" which is not softened by the soul. This intensity from the lack of soul-I co-operation can arise at the start of our quest. To avoid being cold and intense, we need to work harder on our soul's agility. This agility is fostered by receiving vivid impressions of things in the world. If we encourage ourselves to think in terms of metaphor, we can enliven our soul through the process of creating images and connections. For example, if we think: 'he is *as strong as a semi-trailer*' or 'this sweater is *as soft as a kitten*', we hold more within our soul than if we had thought: 'he's strong' or 'that's soft'. Likewise if we use adjectives to say: 'that's a *thorny* question', or 'what a *slippery* answer', our listener is enriched by the colour of our associations for the terms 'question' and 'answer'. To use language in this way we let the world touch us and we build connections to other impressions which are stored in our memory.

When we are dull to outer events and unobservant our soul is inflexible, stiff and inactive which is the cause of our "I" being cold and intense.

When our soul is active we can process information wisely.

The full capacity of our soul is available to everyone who becomes conscious of the forces working in their soul. Intelligence is not a matter of IQ; it is about having an agile soul and an active, mature I-connection. Therefore the capacity for intelligence is at everyone's disposal. If someone appears to us to be less intelligent we will find the cause not in their brain's capacity but in the way their "I" is able to work into feeling, thinking and willing in their soul. It can be observed that a person who uses their will to pass their university exams may still not be able to apply their knowledge in an agile way. This is because they focus on certain parts of their soul and exclude others. Using sheer will to accomplish something does nothing for the teamwork of our soul and "I".

Once our soul is awake and we are actively engaged in the world certain choices arise. We can:

1. Do everything to benefit self which is selfish and egotistical—
'me first';
2. Enhance ourselves to enhance the world - the balanced solution;
3. Deny self to benefit the world - altruistic and also egotistical.

It is more common for people do everything to benefit self (1) or deny self to benefit the world (3); it is not so common to work on both their self and the world (2); this requires a strong I-connection.

Exercise

Spend some time thinking about the following: that the "I" is expressed in our *personality*, the expression of which is an evolving thing. Our *character* is the result of the influence of the "I" on our soul. Our *talent* resides in our "I".

5. BECOMING MORE CONSCIOUSNESS OF OUR "I"

a. Healing our connection with the world

Our "I" remains inactive unless it has an object to focus on; the external stimulus engages the "I" to be active. If we are totally withdrawn within ourselves, focussed on our own issues, and the external world does not touch us, then we are not connected to our "I".

> *When we are confident, our "I"*
> *fills the space around us and we have no fear.*

If we can enlarge the sense of self to encompass our immediate environment we will feel more confident. It is when we cannot contact our sense of self that we can feel anxious and fearful.

An isolated person does not engage with the world through their soul. They cannot embrace what is currently happening and instead retreat within their soul. They will be functioning from the lower regions of their soul and their I-connection will be weak. This leaves them detached from others and the world.

Isolation can be a two-way experience

However, it is also the case that others can isolate a person when they are perceived to be different. A person who does not act as we expect them to can make us uncomfortable and we push them away. We reject them because we are unable to engage with their soul forces. This means that each time they reach out the rejection causes them to retreat into the lower soul regions. We cannot always blame the person who is isolated; they are not always the sole cause of their isolation. These situations can be overcome through a mature I-connection. Through our "I" we have much in common with others; it is because of our soul that differences arise.

b. Healing through finding the patterns of our life

When we observe the patterns that arise in our daily life we can decide to consciously involve our "I" when these situations repeat themselves. We enrich the soul when we see that it is not by chance or coincidence that we encounter people and situations in our life. Our behavioural patterns seem to attract the same situations until we can change them.

Seeing the hidden connections in life enriches the soul.

Our "I" can seem shadow-like at those times when we can only operate out of the lower soul regions. Even though we know we have an "I" we do not always express ourselves through it. When we do strengthen our I-connection we can see the hidden connections in life, whether in complex issues or small 'coincidences'. If we set aside time each day to be with ourselves, there is an opportunity to reflect upon seeming 'coincidence', to explore all connections and possibilities and find the patterns in our life. This will assist our soul to be livelier and more willing to involve our "I".

c. Healing through taking responsibility for our own development

We need a direct experience of how our soul is our personal instrument. It is *our* inner life that we nurture, and its vitality depends on *us*. It doesn't depend on our parents, our friends; only on us. We are born with an innate ability to develop the relationship between our soul and our "I". It is often the people who have the greatest obstacles in their early life who have the greatest relationship with their "I" as they progress in life. Perhaps this is the origin of the folk wisdom that obstacles are 'character building'.

*We develop independence and we become
more self-assured through our I-connection.*

We also need to give some attention to our vision for the future. Even though, in this modern world, it may be difficult to imagine the future, creating some vision for the future keeps our soul bright and awake. The vision will actually come to us from our "I", it is our soul that prefers things the way they are.

One exercise to strengthen our I-connection is to review our day in reverse order. This assists us to control our *desires* and guide them through

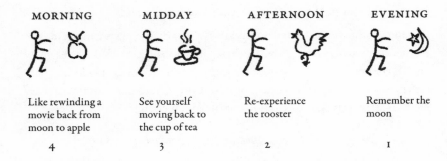

MORNING	MIDDAY	AFTERNOON	EVENING
Like rewinding a movie back from moon to apple	See yourself moving back to the cup of tea	Re-experience the rooster	Remember the moon
4	3	2	I

the soul to fulfilment in a higher way when we followed the process described in chapter 3. As we move quickly backwards through the day's events we will reach points where we want to stop and experience what happened in more detail. These will be times when our soul and "I" did not connect properly and our feeling, thinking and will were out of balance.

Daily exercises to become aware of our soul and "I"

The soul is a living, breathing, flexible thing and it needs continuous exercise. An unfit soul is a rigid soul, it can't move easily. The basic requirement is to be energetic in the whole of our soul as often as possible. Not floating on the waves of feeling where we could be struck by a big ship.

Here are some ways for us to become familiar with our soul's disposition and give our soul a work out – these are like the weights and the treadmill in the soul gym. If we take one of these exercises as the focus for

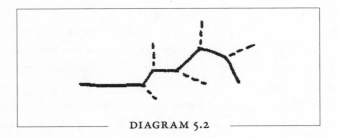

DIAGRAM 5.2

each day of the month, at the end of the month will be a changed person. It is surprising how easily they become an integral part of life.

Awareness of existing patterns

1. Distinguish between past, present and future – see the future coming towards us not us moving towards the future. Look back and see the alternative decisions we could have made (whether for a day, a year or the whole of life). We can do it by drawing a map as shown in diagram 5.2. Move along a path, come to a fork, label the paths, see how we made a decision to go down one path, and then we come to another fork and so on.

2. Realise that re-experiencing an experience IS the soul life. Every time we remember something we are doing it in our soul. If it is something that bugs us, torments us, we are in the lower regions of the soul. We can only resolve it by raising it up and allowing the "I" to shine into the situation and influence our attitude. Then we can see how useful the experience was.

3. Develop strengths in areas of the soul that take us over. Old patterns can be replaced with a new pattern. It only takes a week of effort to create a new pattern. It is not good to do things the same way all the time; then our actions are too automatic and unconscious.

4. Practice being impartial by being open to something that we don't quite agree with. We don't have to discredit the ideas of others, nor do we have to accept them as our own, but we can be open to them. Even more helpful is to experience the ideas of others as if they were our own. We will always find some truth in their idea even if we do not agree.

Awareness of the outside world

5. Work out how much we participate in life and where we escape from life. Are we like a snail withdrawing its feelers each time the world touches us? Are we more likely to do this in some situations and not others?

6. Try not to see people and things in the outer world as objects; try to build a living connection with them, they are an integral part of our life.

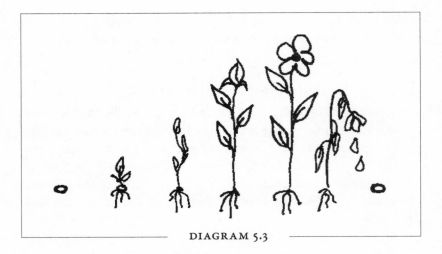

DIAGRAM 5.3

This includes things and people that annoy us.

7. Think of the life process of a plant: seed, leaf, roots, stem, flower, fruit and seed. Grow a seed in a saucer with cotton wool and observe.

8. Observe the living and dying processes in the outer world. Recognise in the things that we see that which is coming into being and that which is fading away. Look at a plant and recognise which stage it is in; seed, shoot, bud, flower, and back to seed again which will repeat the cycle in the following year. These are the things that occupied Goethe's mind as he did his research.

9. When we observe things in the outside world consider where things are in the cycle—not only nature. Apply it to people and processes. Is the process just beginning, or is it at the mature phase of the cycle? What is flowering in us and what seed is being produced for the future?

10. Distinguish the perishable from the imperishable. Leave a piece of fruit on the kitchen bench and watch how it perishes. Observe a plant and see the lasting living impulse in a decaying plant. A flowering plant will often flower before it dies because it the flower creates the seed to carry on the species.

11. Place a seed and glass bead that looks like the seed side by side and contemplate the difference between the two. Notice that one contains a perceptible living force.

12. Become more aware that sense impressions become conscious through intersection in our soul—like when we touch one hand with the other, or an aroma reaches our nose, or music reaches our ears.

13. Think about how we experience the world from outside ourselves and how we experience ourselves from inside. Think of the perimeter of our body as larger than our physical body, then the things in our immediate environment are seen from within our being. This is a way to overcome fear.

If we are afraid, say if an intruder came into our house, we can see them as part of our being— if we can—and that they are standing within the regions of our own soul. Imagine doing the same with a spider or some other fearful thing.

This way we see our self as a larger being and things in our immediate environment are inside us not outside us. This is the reality of our being, for our "I" moves around in the world as a much larger part of our being than our physical body. Also, notice the effect this has on the people we meet, they will feel embraced by us.

Awareness of values

14. Recognise and take more notice of the valuable and the genuine rather than the fleeting, the superficial.

15. Try to look for the good, the beautiful and the purposeful in our environment, even in something that does not seem to have a purpose.

16. It is soul strengthening to look up to something or someone, to have a hero. If we can find ways to look up to things and people, have goals and ideals to reach, our soul will be vibrant.

> a. Look up in admiration for others, have a hero.
> b. Look down and be grateful for the things that support us.
> c. Look beside with respect to our co-workers, friends and family.

Awareness of interaction with others

17. Be creative as often as possible by having new thoughts and ideas of our own. As part of the learning process it is all right for our soul to copy

others but at times we must also create out of our own effort. It is not healthy to always feed from other people's ideas and creativity instead of nourishing ourselves with our own creative thinking.

18. Identify where others try to influence us with their ideas etc. and where we do the same. It is important that we have the freedom to reach our own conclusions; the energy involved in this strengthens us. The striving is what benefits our soul.

19. Try to avoid using empty phrases. When we speak we should try to give the other person an experience of the living reality of our words. Since we are presently developing the awareness soul regions, our experience of the reality of what is being communicated matters most, not simply an experience of the actual words. The use of metaphor can assist. Don't say, "How are you?" to a person unless we really care how they are.

20. Examine what we want to say with healthy reason (soul region 2), not with sympathy and antipathy (soul region 1). If we think and speak through our personal feelings, where like and dislike has a strong influence, we are always biased.

Awareness of self

21. Think of our body as a vehicle which is taking us from place to place like a car does.

22. Develop images of things rather than wordy concepts. For example, appreciation is like a flower stretching up towards the sun so that it may itself become sunlight.

23. Try different ways to control our actions. Notice how many of our actions are automatic. Do something a different way, or do something that we would not normally do. This means that we have to make the effort to think about how to do it.

24. Think about how difficult or frustrating it is to do a thing for the first time, and the sense of familiarity when we do it the second time. This is easy to do with computer programmes, for instance.

25. When we are thrown by the ebb and flow of feelings, try to check ourselves and stay centred, even if only for a moment.

26. Strengthen our thinking. Concentrate on one thought, for example, the sky is blue, and fight off other thoughts that try to intrude.

27. If we want to learn something; learn it, sleep on it, learn it again and sleep on it again. This will enhance our memory.

28. If we want to make a decision, think about the issue, sleep on it, the next day think about the issue again. If possible sleep on it for three nights and the resolution will be all the wiser.

29. Try not to treat someone according to the information we received from another person. If a friend tells us that they don't like so-and-so, this does not mean that we will dislike them also.

30. It is better for the soul to experience evenness:

a. Try not to overestimate or underestimate ability. State the situation as it is.

b. Resist being cold, hard, calculating, or being over-heated with enthusiasm but try instead to express a warm embracing.

c. Don't sink into lethargy or apathy nor be fanatical but have caring concern.

Imposed challenges for the soul

As we strengthen our soul we come to realise that our soul actually welcomes life's little dramas. Our soul is strengthened by dealing with unexpected events because it is jolted out of its regular patterns. Although our soul prefers more of the same, it secretly hopes to be released from this repetition. At this stage in our evolution the soul hopes that our "I" will intervene and take things to a different level instead of going down the same old path. Through an act of will we can be creative and introduce something new into the soul. This marks the input of the "I" and sometimes even from the regions above our soul; the spirit.

Get over your soul

Often we need to get over our soul; its repetitive patterns weigh us down and prevent us from expressing our 'self' in a higher way. It is important to work out how to move through all the levels of our self, to see them for what they are, and be able to act accordingly. Like the racing car driver in chapter 3, navigating the bends and curves, the obstacles, changing gears, monitoring the pressure on the accelerator and the brake to move from A to B to speed up the highway.

Then, about winning: if we give it our best shot and we come second we should feel just as elated as the one who comes first. When the "I" connects firmly with our soul we will feel the satisfaction of trying our best. If the soul rules so do feelings of jealousy and failure.

Contemplate the following in the light of all that you have read in this chapter and before. It can give us a real sense of our place in the world.

"In Silence, everything is experienced as "within" but not as "within us". We, along with everything else, are within Silence. Here new laws of perceiving hold. In our ordinary sensing and perceiving we experience things as outside of us, in front of us, to the side of us, above, below, and behind us. The physical body limits our perspectives. When we perceive something while we are in the realm of Silence, we perceive qualities of the interior of things from the place of our own interior being. For example, in ordinary perceiving, the tree that sits outside a window is "over there." As long as we perceive it as "over there" we are not present to the Silence. From within Silence, the boundary between us and the tree becomes diaphanous substance. We are then taken out of the kind of perceiving that knows in advance what it perceives into a way that is present to the unknown. Here, feeling ascends, not emotion, but feeling. It is a new way of know, knowing as artists or musicians know when doing their art."

—from *Silence* by Robert Sardello 2006

To gain a deeper insight into the workings of our soul it is necessary to look in more detail at some other aspects of our being. In the appendix we will look at the way we touch the world and the way the world touches us though our senses. We will investigate the cycles we pass through, our masculinity and femininity, temperaments, consciousness and memory.

APPENDIX

In this section information from many sources has been gathered together which give us further ways to understand our being. These areas will only be touched on briefly and for a greater understanding the works of Rudolf Steiner and those who have researched his work are a fruitful resource.

If we want to be more conscious it is necessary for us to quicken the activity of our soul. Once we start to experience this quickening of the functions of the soul, a new curiosity enters into our life. How does the soul really interact with the world? Does the soul always interact with the body? How do the soul and the body work together? What are bodily functions and what are soul functions? How can I identify the role of the "I"? This is emerging knowledge and the reason why this book is written.

These questions cannot be answered fully with today's scientific knowledge. Only when we explore for ourselves how our own soul works and interacts with our body and spirit will more answers emerge. In other words, this knowledge cannot be mere theory. It cannot be debated. It is human experience. If we can wake ourselves up to a more complete experience of our being the answers to these questions will emerge from within us.

The fundamental point made in this book is that our "I" lives in the world through our senses. When we are born our whole body is one large sense organ. Gradually, as we mature, our senses take on their individual nature. The extent to which these senses are refined and the extent to which these senses are used, depends on our I-connection.

When we consider the nature of our relationship with the outside world we understand that an outer impression, be it a sound, a smell, a colour, an image, is a sense perception. These things press themselves onto our body in various ways through our five sense organs; our nose, our ears, and our eyes, our tongue and our skin.

Our senses are like fingers of the soul.

What happens in our soul when we look at something or when an outer impulse comes to us? First of all we must realise that a sense is a perception through which we obtain knowledge without the help of a mental process, without thinking. So when that perception enters our body, thinking is not involved. We can still call it knowledge, it is still information, but we haven't applied our thinking to it. The outside world comes to us as an impression and then *afterwards* we think about it; thinking comes second. As discussed earlier, sometimes we don't think about it and the impression fades and dies like a rainbow.

This means that our sense organs are the gates of our soul. The outside world enters our body and then our soul is able to act upon it. Thinking, as we know, is a function of the soul which uses the instrument that is our brain. Therefore, the purpose of our senses is to make our soul active. If we are numb to the outside world then our soul is not engaged. This is what occurs when someone is in shock or very ill.

Twelve senses

So when we perceive the outside world this process of perception uses our senses. We can expand on the familiar five senses and show that there are really twelve ways in which we can become aware of ourselves in the world.[1] These twelve ways can be grouped according to feeling, thinking and willing. These twelve senses are: touch, life, self-movement, balance, smell, taste, sight, warmth, hearing, word, thought and the sensing of the other person's "I". We may not all be aware of the full twelve, this will depend on the quality of our I-connection.

The senses also work in teams.

These twelve individual senses function as an integrated whole, working one within the other according to the situation. For example, when we smell food, we experience the memory of the taste of it shortly afterwards. When we have tasted the food, we can compare if it is better or worse than our memory of the taste.

We can divide these twelve senses into groups according to willing[a], feeling[b] and thinking[c]. We can also divide them into senses that we experience *within*[a] us (for example, self-movement), senses that we experience *outside*[b] us (for example, smell) and senses of comprehension or *understanding the world*[c], (for example, meaning). Furthermore, we can divide these into physical senses[a], soul senses[b] and spirit senses[c]. The following is a brief description of each of the senses. If we investigate them ourselves we will discover much more about each of them.

The Willing Senses[a] from WITHIN

These senses give us a sense of ourselves and our place in the world as well as our well-being.

TOUCH We sense the boundaries of our physical body. While this sense interacts with the outside world, the perception that results happens inside our skin. We come into physical contact with the outside world and by doing so become conscious of our self. Touch, in essence, reveals to us whether something is hard or soft.

LIFE The processes of life within us are thirst, hunger, tiredness, wellness, energy. When we experience these things we become inwardly aware of ourselves and that we are a self-enclosed, living being.

SELF MOVEMENT The automatic movements which contribute to our wellbeing such as blinking, breathing, digestion, blood flow, metabolism, awareness of our limb movement. These can respond according to stimulus, for example danger or anxiety.

BALANCE We experience our sense of balance when we stand upright and maintain our balance. For example, we may walk on the deck of a rolling ship without staggering or walk on uneven surfaces without tripping.

The Feeling Senses[b] from WITHOUT

These senses reveal to us the way we touch the world.

SMELL We touch the world through the sense of smell. Through smell, substances reveal their outer nature. When we smell a cup of coffee, it reveals its outer nature to us in the form of gas that fills the air to touch us as it enters our nose.

TASTE Through taste, substances reveal their inner nature to us. When we taste chocolate, we experience the inner nature of it. This gives us an intimate contact with the outside world.

SIGHT While we touch the surface of objects when we look at them, the depth of an object is also revealed to our eyes through colour as well as our understanding of how objects stand in relation to each other.

TEMPERATURE We may think of temperature as being related to the sense of touch. However, this sense is not only about touch, because sensing heat or cold also reveals that the inner quality of an object is the same as the surface quality. If we touch a piece of ice we know that the core of the ice is also cold.

The Thinking Senses[c] for COMPREHENSION

These senses help us to understand the world and our place in it.

HEARING Sound gives us a sense of the inner nature of an outer object. Here the inner nature of a thing speaks to us. When we hear a cricket ball hit a bat we have an understanding of the hardness and density of the ball and the resilience of the wood in the bat.

LANGUAGE Language is regarded as a sense because it shapes and imbues our interaction with the world. Our use of language and tone reveal the inner nature of speech. When we use language, we convey our place within the world and how we position ourselves in relation to our understanding. When we listen to language we ask: Does it make sense of what it refers to?

CONCEPTS Through concepts, we come to an understanding of the thoughts of others, the meaning referred to by the words they use. It is the work of reasoning with concepts that makes the soul active.

"I" With this sense we perceive the "I" of the other person. When we look at each other we know that the other person is another being with an "I", rather than an animal, plant or mineral.

When we meet the outside world our twelve senses separate things into their various components. These may interpenetrate so that, for example, we experience a warm smell or a cold taste. We then unite them so that we can make sense of things. Something can come to us from our environment that involves, say, three senses. We unite all three so we know what to make of the impression. We then process the impression in a sequence: first of all we reach a conclusion, then we make a judgment, then we form a concept and finally we understand. These processes happen within us all the time. The smell and then the taste can become the concept coffee and we understand that we can drink it.

Senses and consciousness

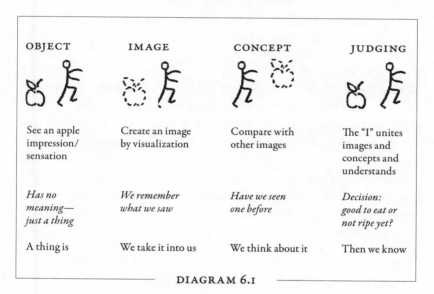

OBJECT	IMAGE	CONCEPT	JUDGING
See an apple impression/ sensation	Create an image by visualization	Compare with other images	The "I" unites images and concepts and understands
Has no meaning— just a thing	*We remember what we saw*	*Have we seen one before*	*Decision: good to eat or not ripe yet?*
A thing is	We take it into us	We think about it	Then we know

DIAGRAM 6.1

When we create the image, it is just that, an image, not the real thing. The apple on the tree is recreated in our mind as a replica. Remember that it is a creative process within us which reconstructs something from the past. Our ability to do this varies in accuracy according to the liveliness of our soul and strength of our I-connection.

Summary of the journey of an outer impression

We receive an impression such as the sight of an apple or the sound of a bee, into our body through our senses. Then our soul makes the sensation, the outer impression, an object of our consciousness. We think 'bee' and according to our past experiences of bees, a mental image is formed. The "I" absorbs and takes possession of the image and we act according to our inner knowledge of bees.

Because the domain of the "I" is the soul and the soul is connected to our body, this is what happens when we perceive:

◇ our *body* absorbs the object through our senses;
◇ our *impulse soul* absorbs the impression, the image;
◇ our *reasoning soul* digests the object and forms knowledge about it, and personalises it;
◇ our *awareness soul* possesses the inner knowledge which the object gives and we comprehend it in relation to the world.

What sort of concepts might we form at this point? We may think in relation to our body that the bee will sting us. We could also think of the bee in relation to the world, of the honey the bee produces, and of the importance of the bee in the process of plant pollination. If the bee didn't enter into us any further than the impulse region of the soul we would not know what to make of it. Just as the Australian Aboriginal woman thought the truck that she saw was a moving rock. Perhaps the bee escapes our notice entirely, because we are unobservant. If the bee then stings us, it is as if it is saying: hey, I am here, notice me, become conscious of me!

The role of the "I" in comprehending the world

The "I" creates order out of the chaos in our being.

The "I" is the active agent that must conquer the currents and forces of the soul and body—it does this by penetrating into them. The forces of our body and soul can whirl around in a chaotic way, which can be overwhelming. The "I" creates order out of this chaos by penetrating into these forces and controlling them to the degree that it can. If we are overwhelmed, it means that the "I" could not penetrate enough to create harmony.

Sometimes the "I" can tunnel too deeply and become too entangled in feeling, thinking and willing. If this happens, the "I" does not have enough mobility and we find it difficult to be objective. Feeling is then likely to dominate and we can respond in unhelpful ways.

Therefore it is a matter of how conscious we can be of our feeling, thinking and will. In the "I" the union of images and concepts is produced. This will obviously be affected by the strength of our I-connection. The continuity of consciousness is only possible because the "I" places images in memory and links them with yesterday's perceptions to form judgments. The soundness of our judging again depends on how conscious we are. If it were just up to our senses, the impressions wouldn't be linked together and we would see everything as if for the first time.

Let the world speak to us.

If we can remain passive towards the things that approach us, they will speak to us. We can do this by preventing our feeling, thinking and willing from becoming too active or too overpowering. If we immediately decide to like or dislike things and form opinions, things that approach us will never yield their secrets. We will only know and understand partially. Then we make decisions with only half the information. It is the same with knowledge; if we are too busy with it, we won't understand it. If we can remain neutral and let it come to us, it will reveal itself more fully. Instant like or dislike shuts the door on possibilities.

On the other hand, to partly use our senses robs us of the complete sensation. Tentativeness usually indicates a weak I-connection.

Cycles in life

We are not born with all the regions of our soul fully functional. The soul and the "I" have to gradually integrate with the body. This becomes obvious when consider the phases of development of a baby, a child, a teenager and an adult. Close observation reveals that development can be divided into an approximate seven-year rhythm. About every seven years of life our expression changes in a number of ways. We could say that something new is born in us each seven years. This change does not occur exactly at the seven year mark; some changes may occur later and others earlier, depending on life's circumstances.

The way we use the soul regions in later life depends on the way we lived the first three cycles, from birth to twenty-one. Here we find the reason for the importance of the 21st birthday.

Below is a brief description of the overall theme of each seven year period. Concepts such as this should not be set in stone; they should arise out of personal discovery:

0-7   Our *physical* body develops. Science tells us that we are continually replacing all the cells in our body so during our first seven years we actually rebuild the body that our mother gave us. Between the ages of one-and-a-half and four our I-connection begins and we have a sense of self, a self-awareness. Memory comes into operation. Our earliest childhood memories only go back to the point when our I began to connect because this is when we first began to engage with the world out of a personal sense of self. Our physical forces are strengthened and made supple and compliant. The transition out of this period is marked by the change of teeth—we lose our inherited teeth and replace them with our own teeth.

7-14   During this cycle our *drives*, the life-forces in our body, dominate. The energy that was used to build up the body is now available to the mind and our ability to think develops. While our thinking develops learning can be greatly assisted through artistic means rather than purely intellectual methods—simply because our thinking is still developing. If in this period of our life we have good role models, people we trust, this will assist us to have courage and initiative when we integrate the reasoning/logic soul regions later in life. Puberty leads the way to the next phase.

14-21   The soul life dawns during this cycle. Our *desires* and passions emerge and we learn to use our own will rather than have it imposed on us by parents and teachers. High ideals and enthusiasm can be imprinted on our soul—although we can be too idealistic and sensitive. The tone of this period is one of experimenting and is largely a struggle with responsibility and emotions. Approximately between 16 and 18 years-of-age the I-connections enters a new phase of development and we are able to work more directly with the "I". This is a crucial time to make decisions about the future and career path. At this time teenagers should really wrestle to think about what they will do in the future. This can be a struggle between laziness and the effort required to think things through thoroughly.

21-28 Now we begin to work on our soul as a free, independent person, we are able to balance our instincts and passions with our experiences in the outer world. Youth fades away. Our character develops as our I-connection continues to strengthen according to our effort. The urge arises to do something meaningful. It is in this period that the extent of our individuality reveals itself. People who marry during this period can find that the relationship ends when they reach 28.

28-35 The *impulse* soul region develops. The emphasis is to control the feeling levels; like and dislike are strong in us. We can make some dramatic changes in our life a few years into this period. We have a greater sense of purpose. We re-experience our 14-21 years but in a more refined way. What happened in those years can affect this period. The cause of any difficulties may be found there.

35–42 We develop the *reasoning* regions of the soul, our thinking matures, we become more self-contained and more self-assured. 35 is seen as a midpoint in our lives. Our inner life deepens and we are more reflective. This is the time when we may wonder about the meaning of life and about our true nature. We take stock of, and assess, what has been of value in our life so far. The eternal nature of things can become more important. Creativity and achievement reaches its peak. If we had good role models between 7 and 14 then we will show a lot of initiative now. At the end of this period some people can feel that they have been living a lie, up till now.

42-49 The third region of the soul develops. Our *awareness* is heightened. We observe the world more carefully and we interact with the world through the knowledge and experience we have developed throughout our life. Any unkindness, pain or distress that occurred in the first 7 years of life can be experienced here as obstacles. At the end of this period we can experience a sense of freedom.

49-56 What transpires in this cycle depends very much on the preceding cycles. There can be a heightened sense of freedom, a quiet confidence or it can be a real wilderness. It can be a period of turning away from the world, away from the familiar frameworks. Each one experiences this period differently according to the foundation laid in the previous cycles.

56-63 Now we experience a fullness, we feel a need to give back to the world. We may take up study or put our energy into achieving something quite different from the achievements in our life so far. We may experiment more with life. You will often hear people in this age bracket say, "I have never done this before." On the other hand we may be full of regret and disappointment.

Our experiences affect the way each cycle comes to expression in us. So the cycles and the soul regions and our I-connection shed light on the way we differ from each other. This is one way to explain how two people born on the same day, with the same astrological sign can be so different; a person can develop one region of the soul more fully than another given the prevailing circumstances. It could be the disposition of the "I" that leans towards one soul region or the other. If the "I" connects more strongly in the impulse soul it will then shine out its influence from there to the other soul regions. There will be an overtone of feeling. If the "I" connects more strongly in the reasoning soul region, then thinking will dominate. This can often be at the expense of feeling and so a cold and calculating person may be the result. The ideal is that the "I" connects in a modulated way through all regions of the soul and irradiates the soul from the awareness region.

Masculinity and femininity

It can also be observed that the soul expresses itself through masculinity and femininity. As we move through the seven year cycles we oscillate between masculine and feminine expressions. It has been observed that a female child between the ages of 0 and 7 usually expresses herself through

MALES		FEMALES		CYCLE
0 – 7 years	Feminine	0 – 7 years	Masculine	Body
7 – 14 years	Masculine	7 – 14 years	Feminine	Drives
14 – 21 years	Feminine	14 – 21 years	Masculine	Desires
21 – 28 years	Masculine	21 – 28 years	Feminine	"I"
28 – 35 years	Feminine	28 – 35 years	Masculine	Impulse soul
35 – 42 years	Masculine	35 – 42 years	Feminine	Reasoning soul
42 – 49 years	Feminine	42 – 49 years	Masculine	Awareness soul
49 – 56 years	Masculine	49 – 56 years	Feminine	
56 – 63 years	Feminine	56 – 63 years	Masculine	

her masculine levels. In her next cycle between 7 and 14 she is usually more feminine. Similarly a 25 year old female normally has overtones of masculinity and can be drawn to do things that are not so feminine. A 25 year old male could be softer than he will be when he is 30. Test this out for yourself.

At this stage in the history of mankind we can observe a new phenomenon; a blurring of the boundaries between masculine and feminine. The human race is becoming more androgynous. Sometimes it is hard to tell if a person walking down the street is male or female. So today, the masculine and feminine expression through the cycles is not as delineated. The rise of same sex relationships is another example of the changing roles of the sexes.

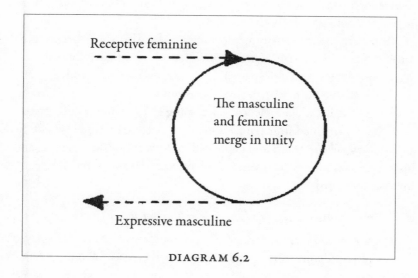

Receptive feminine

The masculine
and feminine
merge in unity

Expressive masculine

DIAGRAM 6.2

The eastern notion of yin and yang can now be seen to merge into a unity within the soul. If we use the input/output diagram we can see the three part process, it is a rhythmic breathing process, the feminine is receptive and passive receiving into herself, and meeting in union with, the expressive masculine force.

The diminishing difference between the sexes means that there is a greater balance within us. Today there are many issues arising from the changing nature of the masculine and feminine within the human being.

Many girls in their twenties are now saying that they would rather be single than deal with the boys their age. Some people whose work involves assessing these females notice that they are becoming more masculine than ever in this cycle. In the workplace their performance can equal their male counterparts. It will be interesting to see the present generation of twenty-something when they are in their forties. We may see that women will take the lead in the corporate world more naturally by then.

Temperament

When we consider all the different ways we can express ourselves it becomes clear that there are different types of consciousness and different degrees of being conscious. Consciousness, or awareness, is what the third region of the soul is all about.

There are many tools to map consciousness. The Myers-Briggs Type Indicator is one modern method. There are many other indicators and philosophies by which we can analyse the way we express ourselves.

The idea that we have different dispositions or temperaments arose at the time of Plato when logic was developing in the human soul. In 200 AD Galen identified four temperaments or personality types which he called: *melancholic* or sad and depressed; *phlegmatic* or slow moving and apathetic; *sanguine* or warm and pleasant; and *choleric* or quick to react and hot tempered.

Temperament is the fundamental colouring of our personality.

Temperament indicates the mood of a person. Temperament is displayed in our physical constitution and it provides the basis for our soul life. We have said that our personality, our individuality, reveals the way we express our "I". If someone asks us what our "I" is, the best answer we can give is that it is our personality. So temperament is closely tied to our "I" and it colours our consciousness, our awareness. We could say that temperaments are coloured glasses through which we see the world. Our temperament reveals a balance between our own qualities and what we receive from our parents. Through our "I" we merge our own qualities with the influence from our parents and this produces our temperament.

There are four basic temperaments or personality types although most people have one basic temperament with parts of the others mixed in. It is better, if we want to work on ourselves in this area, to focus on the temperament that is dominant in us rather than try to build up the ones we are less inclined to express. The aim is that while we will inevitably express the dominant temperament we must work toward expressing the others in harmony with it.

1. MELANCHOLIC—TO BE SAD AND DEPRESSED

If we have a melancholic temperament, we will be pensive, depressed, sad and despondent, and we will feel pain. This temperament is expressed when the *physical body* dominates our being. We feel as though our physical body resists our inner sense of well-being, our liveliness, and our purposeful striving.

In childhood the melancholic temperament responds best to people who have known their own pain. As an adult, it is helpful for a melancholic person to seek out life's pain, although the instinct is to avoid it. Through compassion for others we redirect our suffering outward and in this way we can experience another person's fate and pain. Unfortunately the melancholic can often not be sensitive to other people's pain because they focus on their own misery. Mental problems can arise if they remain too focussed on their own pain.

When balanced, this temperament is able to be bright, cheerful and optimistic.

The element of earth is connected with this temperament.

2. PHLEGMATIC—TO BE INDIFFERENT AND SLOW MOVING

If we have a phlegmatic temperament, we will be matter-of-fact, indifferent, sluggish, apathetic or placid. We have an inner sense of comfort and we are timid. In those with this temperament the *drives* and life processes which are controlled by the glandular system dominate. The focus is on what is happening inside us and the world passes us by; we are not entirely in touch with our surroundings. This temperament manifests itself in a static, indifferent appearance; a way of walking that is loose-jointed and awkward, as well as in plumpness (for fat is due largely to the activity of the drives in our body).

As a child we are not very interested in what others are doing. This continues in the adult with a phlegmatic temperament. To balance this, we should expand the range of our interests and involvement with others so that their enthusiasm assists us to overcome our indifference. When balanced this temperament is much more energetic.

The element of water is associated with this temperament.

3. SANGUINE—TO BE WARM AND CONFIDENT

If we have a sanguine temperament, we are cheerful, hopeful, optimistic, pleasant, and confident; this is reflected in our light, springy step. This temperament is expressed when our desires dominate. The nervous system has the upper hand. Feelings play a strong role; feelings and sensations flow one after the other and we find it hard to stop and focus on one sensation before moving onto the next. We are mobile, expressive, lively and changeable in both feelings and behaviour. Our inner liveliness is expressed in every outer detail, for example, in a slender form, a delicate bone structure, red cheeks or lean muscles.

As a child with a sanguine temperament, we need to experience the love and admiration for a personality, say a teacher, to anchor us. As adults we can tend towards flightiness, uncertainty, or obsessiveness, all of which are induced by a constant stream of sensations. The sanguine's short attention span can be counteracted by setting goals that require thought and planning.

When balanced, this temperament allows the "I" to connect more deeply in our being and we develop a deeper interest in things.

The element of air is associated with this temperament.

4. CHOLERIC—TO BE IRRITABLE AND QUICK TO REACT

If we are of a choleric temperament, we can be irritable, bad tempered or angry. Here the "I" dominates. The will is strong and we can be aggressive and want our own way.

As a child with a choleric temperament, we must learn to control our temper. Controlling our temper is necessary so that we develop into maturity, or we will become isolated. If we are irritable, we are also susceptible to being led by others instead of using our own inner resources. Developing respect and esteem for a natural authority gives us balance and calmness of soul. Aggressiveness and wilfulness can be balanced with a concern for others. It is the restraining influence of the "I" that provides the balance.

This temperament is associated with the element of fire.

What is consciousness?

Another way to know ourselves better is to have a greater understanding of our consciousness. Consciousness proceeds from the way we receive outer impressions and the way we respond to these. Consciousness differs between people; each person's soul colours things in a variety of ways.

Unlike our body, which is difficult to change (as anyone trying to lose weight will know), our consciousness is mobile and can change more easily. The decision to change it is ours.

Self-awareness is about connectedness to self and the world.

The "I" possesses self-consciousness, but the world works to make us unconscious. Self-consciousness is, of course, self-awareness. The quality of our consciousness is governed by the way in which our "I" is connected both to our inner being and to the outer world. This connection is a fluctuating thing according to the development of our soul regions. Sometimes we can control the connection, at other times we have no control. However, we must have the connection—with self as well as the outside world, not just with one or the other.

It is worth noting that many self-awareness courses really only work to make us aware of our lower self which is only a reflection of our Real Self—usually a weak reflection. These courses promise us happiness and fulfilment of wishes and longings; all the things that the lower soul seeks at the expense of the "I".

The three levels of consciousness

With all that in mind let's look again at consciousness. We can divide consciousness broadly into three levels.

⋄ Ordinary daily consciousness which we experience when we are awake and alert.

◇ Semi-consciousness which we experience as dreams or sub-consciousness.
◇ Unconsciousness which we can experience as dreamless sleep.

CONSCIOUSNESS	SEMI-CONSCIOUSNESS	UNCONSCIOUSNESS
Awake	Dreaming	Dreamless sleep
Thinking	Feeling	Willing

Compare this table with diagram 3.3 which shows how our soul processes work.

Remember that our ordinary consciousness experiences the world through our senses. We see a rose but we can have no effect with our ordinary consciousness on the growing, blooming and withering of the rose; only nature can do that. Our ordinary consciousness has no power over us either. We cannot make ourselves taller or shorter, thinner, healthy or unhealthy with our ordinary consciousness.

The sub-conscious or semi-conscious levels of our being

Only when we engage our semi-conscious levels can we affect ourselves, and then we can only affect our soul. As we know, this is where likes and dislikes operate. This is where our dreamy feelings mingle with our awakened thinking. Remember that we can only guide our feelings whereas we can change our thinking.

In this middle region of consciousness, all sub-conscious impulses affect everything connected with our *drives*: our blood, our breathing, our warmth. Here is the region where the health of our body and soul are determined. What lives in our sub-conscious levels is ours to control (although sometimes we are lead to believe that we can have no influence here).

We decide what fills our sub-consciousness.

Our sub-conscious levels are simply less conscious than our conscious levels. In other words, they are just below consciousness. Our conscious mind continually feeds our sub-consciousness by sending down to it those daily experiences that we choose to. It is important to realise that we can choose how this is done. So if we can choose what is placed there, we can choose to replace what is there. The best way to do this is to become continually more conscious and aware.

The way our experiences are passed to the sub-conscious levels either creates or depletes our energy. Our circulation is affected; our blood, breathing and warmth are either energised or constricted. In this way the conscious mind either enlivens or stifles the life of the soul. This is because we deposit our feelings and emotions into our sub-conscious, where they are either constructive or destructive. That is our choice.

Take the example of telling a lie. If a lie slips out in our interaction with others and we immediately feel bad about it, this gives energy to our sub-conscious levels. If we take pleasure in the lie, because through it we gained advantage over someone, it is as if part of us has been eaten away, atrophied. In this way we can corrupt our blood, our circulation, our breathing and the area of our being where our drives arise. We may then experiences illnesses in these areas.

Bad feelings, like taking pleasure in lying, definitely cause atrophy. Good sincere feelings give life. If we want to change what we have already deposited in our sub-conscious, we replace it with good sincere feelings. It will soon be evident that it does work.

Awareness of incidents that affect our life

Our consciousness is changed in many and various ways throughout our life and there are a myriad of ways to test this.

If some event happens that changes our life completely, this new thing absorbs our whole attention. For example, if we enter into a serious relationship, our soul enjoys this new thing and keeps away all the unpleasant things that we might have continued to experience if the change hadn't happened, if we hadn't entered into the relationship.

Sudden changes can be traced back to an earlier cause.

For a period of time, perhaps one or two years, we are absorbed in the enjoyment of the new relationship but then when it becomes second nature, the feelings and sentiments that penetrated our soul one or two years before the change, come to the surface in a new way. We can change completely for seemingly no apparent reason and others may wonder what on earth happened!

Now let us suppose that two years before we entered into the relationship, we had a huge fight with our best friend and we haven't spoken to them since. About two years into the new relationship we may experience the feeling of unpleasantness that we felt about the fight with our best friend. This is the recapitulation of our soul's mood as it was two years before the change when we entered into the relationship that we now experience. Put these ideas to work in your life to see if they apply.

Another example would be becoming involved in an activity or an organisation and devoting ourselves to it. It could be sport or course of study. When we begin, it is so exciting and consuming. Then suddenly, two or three years, later the previous issues that this new interest distracted us from rise up again. We probably won't know what they are, but we can trace them back to two or three years before we became involved with the sport or study.

A colleague was having relationship problems, got into drugs, lost his job and licence (drug related), was ordered to attend a rehab, got clean, and went to live on a Hare Krishna organic farm. A couple of years later I met him in the Hare Krishna restaurant and hardly recognised him, because he had been living this outstandingly healthy life compared to before. I was so pleased to see him well and congratulated him on his engagement to another member of the Krishna group. A few months later, I went into the restaurant and when I asked after him I found he had broken up with his fiancé, left the group and was back into drugs. His friends were extremely upset and couldn't understand what happened. I thought how weird it was the way he just stepped sideways and then right back into the same place he left as if nothing happened in between. I have seen this a number of times with people entering communities of different sorts, so I always thought it was to do with entering a different group consciousness that lost its pull when one was used to it, but this is another explanation.

If we become aware of the cycles in our life and the cycles of activity within these cycles we will understand more about ourselves and be strengthened. When we look at the events in our life, by establishing when turning points occur, we can count back and find the cause of the present change in life. This is very useful in understanding certain soul moods or a difficulty in life. If we find ourselves disturbed and uncertain, then counting back may reveal the cause.

Memory

Understanding the way memory works also provides us with more self-knowledge. As we know, the ability to remember varies from person to person. The ability to remember has evolved along with soul development. We can see signs of this in the fact that in earlier times stones and monuments were set in place to mark an event or an occasion. Today this is not so important or even necessary. Our life is full of memories.

Memories are refreshed in two ways:

1. BY SENSE IMPRESSIONS We may have forgotten something that hap-pened years and years ago until we see it again, until it enters us from out-side and we compare what we see with the images and concepts stored within us. If it was a difficult experience, we may now be able to revisit it in a more objective way.

When I was in my thirties I was sitting in the doctor's waiting room, when I noticed an unusual wide but narrow window up near the ceiling. In an instant I was transported back in memory to being locked in my bedroom as a young child when I had been naughty. I had not remembered it once until now, seeing that particular type of window brought the incident back into my memory.

2. BY REFRESHING THE EXPERIENCE WITHIN US We often do this when an unpleasant incident has occurred. We bring it back to life again and again, when really we should be moving on. This is when we must practice forgetfulness. How many things do we resuscitate when they really should be allowed to die? The only way to do is to refuse to think about it. Every time the memory comes back, we need to say, "No, I am not going there." If we can pull back from it, even just a little bit, we can congratulate ourselves. It is a sign that we are gaining control over our soul's automatic functions.

The less conscious we are of things, the lower we sink into our soul. We carry within us a lot of things that we are not conscious of: gifts, talents, understandings and experiences—both good and bad. If our soul is active, we can be less fearful of what lies in our sub-conscious memory because a vital soul with strong I-connection can deal with it. The active soul flushes out any unwanted experiences, purposefully forgets them, and intentionally says, "No, I am not thinking about that now; it is not coming into my consciousness." An unhealthy soul often dwells on such things.

This raises the question about what we tell friends and therapists. Do we sometimes speak of things which should never be spoken? When we speak about things that are better forgotten we enliven them.

One of the extraordinary things about memory is how siblings re-member the same event differently. This can be explained by the different way we each develop our soul and nurture our I-connection.

Exercise

Think of a past event, let it live in your soul. See how it is a different experience than when you had the experience the first time. We can never re-experience the past exactly as it was, we can only re-member it. Notice how you have to add the emotions into the situation, but now these emotions are less intense than when you first had the experience.

Now think of a future event you are looking forward to. Notice how your emotions rise up automatically as you look forward to this planned event. The stronger the emotions the more steps you will take towards the event. Also notice how you have to reign in your emotions to experience patience.

The physical body

Finally, to round off, a bit about the physical body; it is born, it lives through life and then it dies. When we see the body of friend or loved one who has died, we must face the truth that the person we knew is no longer there in the body.

To maintain life our body must have air to breathe, food to eat, warmth, love and a purpose. While it lives it has three modes of operation: it is awake, it is half-asleep/dreaming or fully asleep. Compare the sleeping body with the dead body—there is something similar and there is something different. The difference is that the sleeping body maintains its shape, its form. The dead body quickly looses its shape because the life forces leave and it begins to shrink. The person we knew has left.

Now consider a piece of fruit. Each day as it sits in the fruit bowl it shrinks and then it starts to rot. This is because it is losing the life force given to it from the tree on which it grew. If we left it on the tree it would keep its shape for much longer. So it is obvious that there is a force that gives life and shape. We can call this is our life body or our *drive* to live. A similar *driving* force in the human body tells us to eat and to sleep. The body stays alive and does not die because it has the vital processes that are necessary for life which are breathing, warming, nourishing, secreting, maintaining, growing and reproducing. When we sleep these processes are reduced, when they shut down, we die.

When we sleep the life force remains within us but our consciousness leaves us. Most of our senses shut down especially sight and touch; smell and hearing remain alert. We are (mostly) motionless, unanimated.

When our consciousness leaves us in sleep our action body leaves. This is the part of our body where conscious motion and emotion happen. This is where our *drives* become *desires* and keep us in their grip until they are fulfilled. See diagram 3.3

It is the soul that keeps these two forces, *drives* and *desires*, connected to the body so that life continues. Therefore by the action of our soul, the body is kept from shrinking and rotting like a piece of fruit. Increasingly we must learn to automatically think of the body as a vehicle for the soul and the "I".

Through all the information presented in this book we have developed a larger picture of how we perceive the world and of our place in it. Nevertheless, the words so far expressed are only useful if they can be experienced personally in our lives. However many useful examples are cited; the ideas will only become a reality in our lives if we continue to notice new and personal examples of the way our soul and "I" are expressed as we go about our daily tasks.

I hope that you have enjoyed this book as much as I have enjoyed researching it. It has been many years in the making. It has certainly changed my life, as I hope it will change yours.

Some Further Reading

By Robert Sardello:
Facing the World with Soul, Lindisfarne/Harper, 1992
Love and the Soul: Creating a Future for Earth,
Harper Collins Publishers. 1995
Freeing the Soul from Fear, Putnam/Riverhead, 1999
By Thomas Moore:
Care of the Soul, Harper Collins Publishers. 1992
By James Hillman:
The Soul's Code: In Search of Character and Calling,
Random House 1996
The Force of Character: And the Lasting Life, Random House 1999
By Gerhard Wehr:
Jung & Steiner, the Birth of a New Psychology,
Anthroposophic Press 2002

Acknowledgements

I would like to express my heartfelt thanks to all those who supported this project and indeed poured their soul and spirit into it. They have been changed which is the richest reward.

Diagrams by Robert John.

FOOTNOTES

1 See the work of Rudolf Steiner and others, as well as test it for yourself.

KRISTINA KAINE has always had a curiosity about what makes people tick. In her own human resources business she developed methods of assessing people on an inner level, so that compatible people could be referred to each other. For more than twenty-five years she also studied what others have to say about the human soul and spirit. This book is the result of this research, experience and observation. From her own quest to find the "I", the Real Self at the centre of the soul, the author provides a thoughtful and practical guide to the greatest of all human quests: to know self. The work of *I Connecting* has proved a liberating, thought-provoking and revealing experience for readers as well as participants in the Soul Questing workshops that have developed to support the work of this groundbreaking book.

THE SCHOOL OF SPIRITUAL PSYCHOLOGY

A Center for Creative Service

THE SCHOOL OF SPIRITUAL PSYCHOLOGY is a center of learning and research designed to benefit society as a whole by fostering care for soul and spirit in individual life in conjunction with the renewal of culture as the meeting point between the human heart and the world. This enterprise focuses on more than technical training, intellectual comprehension, or individual inner development of a private nature. The programs and activities of the School serve the formation of capacities for consciously experiencing qualities of soul and spirit in oneself, in the profession and work one practices, in home life, community, and in the larger world. The School has been in operation since 1992 and serves people from all walks of life. In 2004, the School moved to a new center in Benson, North Carolina, near Raleigh. The School operates a program in Sacred Service, a program in Spirit Healing, and Caritas: Caring for those who have Died. The School's website is *www.spiritualschool.org*. The School also publishes a semiannual online journal that can be found at *www.sophiajournal.org*.